Indiana Core (CASA) Study Guide:

Test Prep and Practice Questions for the Core Academic Skills Assessment

Printed in the United States of America

Table of Contents

Free *From Stress to Success* DVD from Trivium Test Prep

Dear Customer,

Thank you for purchasing from Trivium Test Prep! Whether you're looking to join the military, get into college, or advance your career, we're honored to be a part of your journey.

To show our appreciation (and to help you relieve a little of that test-prep stress), we're offering a **FREE**
***From Stress to Success* DVD by Trivium Test Prep**. Our DVD includes 35 test preparation strategies that will help keep you calm and collected before and during your big exam. All we ask is that you email us your feedback and describe your experience with our product. Amazing, awful, or just so-so: we want to hear what you have to say!

To receive your **FREE *From Stress to Success* DVD**, please email us at 5star@triviumtestprep.com. Include
"Free 5 Star" in the subject line and the following information in your email:

1. The title of the product you purchased.

2. Your rating from 1 – 5 (with 5 being the best).

3. Your feedback about the product, including how our materials helped you meet your goals and ways in which we can improve our products.

4. Your full name and shipping address so we can send your FREE *From Stress to Success* DVD.

If you have any questions or concerns please feel free to contact me directly.

Thank you, and good luck with your studies!

Alyssa Wagoner
Quality Control
alyssa.wagoner@triviumtestprep.com

Introduction

Congratulations on continuing your education as you continue to prepare for becoming an educator! Before we get into the test content, we're sure you have questions – everybody does. "How hard is the exam?" "Can I pass on my first try?" "What if I don't? Can I take it again?" "What is even *on* the test?"

Don't worry! We have the answers to all of these questions and more.

While the exam isn't easy, proper planning and preparation can help ensure your success. Sure, you can take the exam again if you fail; but our goal is to give you the keys to outsmarting the exam – the first time around. These first few pages will detail everything you'll need to know about the exam, before leading you into the review material. So get ready to take some notes. Pace yourself. And above all, remember that you are taking the right first step in furthering your career.

Registering for the Exam

This can be done via telephone or computer.

By Phone: Phone registration is only available in "emergency" situations, and is not applicable for "regular" or "late" registrations. Regular and Late registrations must be done by computer.

By Computer: Available 24 hours a day and 7 days a week, simply visit www.in.nesinc.com and find your way to "internet registration" tab. Please note that registrations must be completed by 5:00pm to count for that day. Follow the step-by-step instructions to register, make necessary payment, and confirmation of your registration.

Testing Fees

Even if no additional fees are assessed, knowing that you'll be paying a lot your hard-earned money is an additional incentive to do your best on the exam. Re-taking the test will require you to pay the same fees again – not properly preparing can have expensive consequences!

- The test fee is $38 per subtest, but please note that test centers may at their discretion charge additional fees, so you must check beforehand!

What's on the Exam?

Reading: 40 multiple-choice questions

Mathematics: 40 multiple-choice questions

Writing: 42 multiple-choice questions, 1 constructed-response assignment

How Much Time is Allotted for the Exam?

Reading: 75 minutes

Mathematics: 75 minutes

Writing: 105 minutes

How is the Exam Scored?

You will be scored on a range of 100 to 300 points, with a passing score being 220 per subtest or greater.

Test Day

You MUST Bring

As you head to the testing center, don't forget to bring your ID and any necessary documentation, as well as your Admission Ticket.

You May NOT Bring

Basically, if it's not your Admission Ticket, ID, or any approved device, you can't have it with you. Specifically, you can't bring these items into the testing room:

1. Cell phones, smartphones, or PDAs.
2. Any electronic recording, photographic, or listening device.
3. Food, drink, or tobacco products.
4. Personal items (purses, backpacks, etc.).
5. Paper, pencils, notes, reference material, etc.
6. Weapons of any type.

As if those precautions were not enough, you can also expect to be fingerprinted and/or photographed after entering the testing facility. You may be asked to undergo a quick scan from a metal detecting device before being allowed into the testing room. Additionally, you may be asked to sign a waiver stating that you understand the test administration will be videotaped.

In the event that you object to any of these security measures, you will not be allowed to test.

After the Test

Your test scores will be reported to you, as well as the institution(s) listed when you registered. Check your "test dates" calendar online to see when score reports will be available.

Scores are sometimes delayed if there is a problem with the processing or if there is a new computer test being administered. Your scores could also be delayed if there are problems with your payment, or if you have any outstanding balance.

Unofficial Test Results at a Computer-Based Test Center

At the end of your test, you'll get an "unofficial score". Keep in mind that these scores are not valid for reporting as an official score. You will get your official recorded score at a later date that is valid for use in official capacities.

Chapter 1: Reading

On the Reading section of the **CASA**, you'll have to read passages and answer questions about their content. You may have to identify the main idea of the passage or determine what new information could be added to the passage to bolster the author's argument.

Reading

The **CASA** Reading section assesses your ability to summarize, interpret, and draw conclusions about both non-fiction and fiction passages. On the test, you will read both types of passages; specific questions may ask about the following:

- the main idea of a passage
- the role of supporting details in a passage
- adding supporting details to a passage
- the structure of a passage
- the author's purpose
- logical inferences that can be drawn from a passage
- comparing passages
- vocabulary and figurative language

The questions more broadly fall under four general question types:

Main Idea: A question may directly or indirectly ask you about the main idea of a passage. Summarizing it briefly in your own words or reviewing the first few paragraphs will help you identify the main idea and narrow down your answer choices.

About the Author: These questions ask about the author's attitude, thoughts, and opinions. To determine the correct response, pay attention to context clues in the text. The answer may not be explicitly stated but instead conveyed in the overall message.

Passage Facts: To answer these questions correctly, you must distinguish between facts and opinions presented in the passage. You may also be asked to identify specific information provided by the author.

Additional Information: These questions ask you to consider what information could be added to or was missing from the passage; they may even provide a fill-in-the-blank option to include a new statement at a certain point in the text. Keep in mind that any additional information should strengthen the author's argument. These questions may also ask in what direction the passage was going; that is, about logical inferences that can be drawn from the text.

Strategies

Despite the different types of questions you will face, there are some strategies for Reading Comprehension that always apply:

- Read the questions before reading the passage. You will save time, as you will know what to look out for as you read.
- Use the process of elimination. Often at least one answer choice in a question is obviously incorrect. After reading the passage, eliminate any blatantly incorrect answer choices to increase your chances of finding the correct answer much more quickly.
- Avoid negative statements. Correct responses tend to be neutral or positive, so if it seems like an answer choice has a negative connotation, it is very likely that the answer is intentionally false.

The Main Idea

The main idea of a text is the author's purpose in writing a book, article, story, etc. Being able to identify and understand the main idea is a critical skill necessary to comprehend and appreciate what you're reading.

Consider a political election. A candidate is running for office and plans to deliver a speech asserting her position on tax reform. The **topic** of the speech—tax reform—is clear to voters, and probably of interest to many. However, imagine that the candidate believes that taxes should be lowered. She is likely to assert this argument in her speech, supporting it with examples proving why lowering taxes would benefit the public and how it could be accomplished. While the topic of the speech would be tax reform, the benefit of lowering taxes would be the **main idea**. Other candidates may have different perspectives on the topic; they may believe that higher taxes are necessary, or that current taxes are adequate. It is likely that their speeches, while on the same topic of tax reform, would have different main ideas: different arguments likewise supported by different examples. Determining what a speaker, writer, or text is asserting about a specific issue will reveal the main idea.

One more quick note: the exam may also ask about a passage's **theme**, which is similar to but distinct from its topic. While a topic is usually a specific *person, place, thing*, or *issue,* the theme is an *idea* or *concept* that the author refers back to frequently. Examples of common themes include ideas like the importance of family, the dangers of technology, and the beauty of nature.

There will be many questions on the exam that require you to differentiate between the topic, theme, and main idea of a passage. Let's look at an example:

Babe Didrikson Zaharias, one of the most decorated female athletes of the twentieth century, is an inspiration for everyone. Born in 1911 in Beaumont, Texas, Zaharias lived in a time when women were considered second-class to men, but she never let that stop her from becoming a champion. Babe was one of seven children in a poor immigrant family, and was competitive from an early age. As a child she excelled at most things she tried, especially sports, which continued into high school and beyond. After high school, Babe played amateur basketball for two years, and soon after began training in track and field. Despite the fact that women were only allowed to enter in three events, Babe represented the United States in the 1932 Los Angeles Olympics, and won two gold medals and one silver for track and field events.

In the early 1930s, Babe began playing golf which earned her a legacy. The first tournament she entered was a men's only tournament; however she did not make the cut to play. Playing golf as an amateur was the only option for a woman at this time, since there was no professional women's league. Babe played as an amateur for a little over a decade, until she turned pro in 1947 for the Ladies Professional Golf Association (LPGA) of which she was a founding member. During her career as a golfer, Babe won eighty-two tournaments, amateur and professional, including the U.S. Women's Open, All-American Open, and British Women's Open Golf Tournament. In 1953, Babe was diagnosed with cancer, but fourteen weeks later, she played in a tournament. That year she won her third U.S. Women's Open. However by 1955, she didn't have the physicality to compete anymore, and she died of the disease in 1956.

The topic of this passage is obviously Babe Zaharias—the whole passage describes events from her life. Determining the main idea, however, requires a little more analysis. The passage describes Babe Zaharias' life, but the main idea of the paragraph is what it says *about* her life. To figure out the main idea, consider what the writer is saying about Babe Zaharias. The writer is saying that she's someone to admire—that's the main idea and what unites all the information in the paragraph. Lastly, what might the theme of the passage be? The writer refers to several broad concepts, including never giving up and overcoming the odds, both of which could be themes for the passage. Two major indicators of the main idea of a paragraph or passage follow below:

- It is a general idea; it applies to all the more specific ideas in the passage. Every other sentence in a paragraph should be able to relate in some way to the main idea.
- It asserts a specific viewpoint that the author supports with facts, opinions, or other details. In other words, the main idea takes a stand.

Example

It's easy to puzzle over the landscapes of our solar system's distant planets—how could we ever know what those far-flung places really look like? However, scientists utilize a number of tools to visualize the surfaces of many planets. The topography of Venus, for example, has been explored by several space probes, including the Russian Venera landers and NASA's Magellan orbiter. These craft used imaging and radar to map the surface of the planet, identifying a whole host of features including volcanoes, craters, and a complex system of channels. Mars has likewise been mapped by space probes, including the famous Mars Rovers, which are automated vehicles that actually landed on the planet's surface. These rovers have been used by NASA and other space agencies to study the geology, climate, and possible biology of the planet.

In addition to these long-range probes, NASA has also used its series of orbiting telescopes to study distant planets. These four massively powerful telescopes include the famous Hubble Space Telescope as well as the Compton Gamma Ray Observatory, Chandra X-Ray Observatory, and the Spitzer Space Telescope. These allow scientists to examine planets using not only visible light but also infrared and near-infrared light, ultraviolet light, x-rays and gamma rays.

Powerful telescopes aren't just found in space: NASA makes use of Earth-bound telescopes as well. Scientists at the National Radio Astronomy Observatory in Charlottesville, VA, have spent decades using radio imaging to build an incredibly detailed portrait of Venus' surface. In fact, Earth-bound telescopes offer a distinct advantage over orbiting telescopes because they allow scientists to capture data from a fixed point, which in turn allows them to effectively compare data collected over long period of time.

Which of the following sentences best describes the main idea of the passage?

A)   It's impossible to know what the surfaces of other planets are really like.

B)   Telescopes are an important tool for scientists studying planets in our solar system.

C)   Venus' surface has many of the same features as the Earth's, including volcanoes, craters, and channels.

D)   Scientists use a variety of advanced technologies to study the surface of the planets in our solar system.

Answer A) can be eliminated because it directly contradicts the rest of the passage, which goes into detail about how scientists have learned about the surfaces of other planets. Answers B) and C) can also be eliminated because they offer only specific details from the passage; while both choices contain details from the passage, neither is general enough to encompass the passage as a whole. Only **answer D)** provides an assertion that is both supported by the passage's content and general enough to cover the entire passage.

Topic and Summary Sentences

The main idea of a paragraph usually appears within the topic sentence. The **topic sentence** introduces the main idea to readers; it indicates not only the topic of a passage, but also the writer's perspective on the topic.

Notice, for example, how the first sentence in the text about Babe Zaharias states the main idea: *Babe Didrikson Zaharias, one of the most decorated female athletes of the twentieth century, is an inspiration for everyone.*

Even though paragraphs generally begin with topic sentences due to their introductory nature, on occasion writers build up to the topic sentence by using supporting details in order to generate interest or build an argument. Be alert for paragraphs when writers do not include a clear topic sentence at all; even without a clear topic sentence, a paragraph will still have a main idea. You may also see a **summary sentence** at the end of a passage. As its name suggests, this sentence sums up the passage, often by restating the main idea and the author's key evidence supporting it.

Example

In the following paragraph, what are the topic and summary sentences?

> The Constitution of the United States establishes a series of limits to rein in centralized power. Separation of powers distributes federal authority among three competing branches: the executive, the legislative, and the judicial. Checks and balances allow the branches to check the usurpation of power by any one branch. States' rights are protected under the Constitution from too much encroachment by the federal government. Enumeration of powers names the specific and few powers the federal government has. These four restrictions have helped sustain the American republic for over two centuries.

The topic sentence is the **first sentence in the paragraph.** It introduces the topic of discussion, in this case the constitutional limits on centralized power. The summary sentence is the last sentence in the paragraph. It sums up the information that was just presented: here, that constitutional limits have helped sustain the United States of America for over two hundred years.

Implied Main Idea

A paragraph without a clear topic sentence still has a main idea; rather than clearly stated, it is implied. Determining the **implied main idea** requires some detective work: you will need to look at the author's word choice and tone in addition to the content of the passage to find his or her main idea. Let's look at an example paragraph.

One of my summer reading books was *Mockingjay*. Though it's several hundred pages long, I read it in just a few days *I was captivated by the adventures of the main character and the complicated plot of the book. However, I felt like the ending didn't reflect the excitement of the story. Given what a powerful personality the main character has, I felt like the ending didn't do her justice.*

Even without a clear topic sentence, this paragraph has a main idea. What is the writer's perspective on the book—what is the writer saying about it?

A)   *Mockingjay* is a terrific novel.

B)   *Mockingjay* is disappointing.

C)   *Mockingjay* is full of suspense.

D)   *Mockingjay* is a lousy novel.

The correct answer is B): the novel is disappointing. The process of elimination will reveal the correct answer if that is not immediately clear. While that the paragraph begins with positive commentary on the book—*I was captivated by the adventures of the main character and the complicated plot of the book*—this positive idea is followed by the contradictory transition word *however.* A) cannot be the correct answer because the author concludes that the novel was poor. Likewise, D) cannot be correct because it does not encompass all the ideas in the paragraph; despite the negative conclusion, the author enjoyed most of the book. The main idea should be able to encompass all of the thoughts in a paragraph; choice D) does not apply to the beginning of this paragraph. Finally, choice C) is too specific; it could only apply to the brief description of the plot and adventures of the main character. That leaves choice B) as the best option. The author initially enjoyed the book, but was disappointed by the ending, which seemed unworthy of the exciting plot and character.

Example

Read the following paragraph:

> Fortunately, none of Alyssa's coworkers has ever seen inside the large filing drawer in her desk. Disguised by the meticulous neatness of the rest of her workspace, the drawer betrayed no sign of the chaos within. To even open it, she had to struggle for several minutes with the enormous pile of junk jamming the drawer, until it would suddenly give way, and papers, folders, and candy wrappers spilled out onto the floor. It was an organizational nightmare, with torn notes and spreadsheets haphazardly thrown on top of each other and melted candy smeared across pages. She was worried the odor would soon waft to her coworker's desks, revealing to them her secret.

Which sentence best describes the main idea of the paragraph above?

A)   Alyssa wishes she could move to a new desk.

B)   Alyssa wishes she had her own office.

C)   Alyssa is glad none of her coworkers know about her messy drawer.

D)   Alyssa is sad because she doesn't have any coworkers.

Clearly, Alyssa has a messy drawer, and C) is the right answer. The paragraph begins by indicating her gratitude that her coworkers do not know about her drawer (*Fortunately, none of Alyssa's coworkers has ever seen inside the large filing drawer in her desk.*) Plus, notice how the drawer is described: *it was an organizational nightmare*, and it apparently doesn't even function properly: *to even open the drawer, she had to struggle for several minutes.* The writer reveals that it has an odor, with *melted candy* inside. Alyssa is clearly ashamed of her drawer and fearful of being judged by her coworkers for it.

Supporting Details
Supporting details provide more support for the author's main idea. For instance, in the Babe Zaharias example above, the writer makes the general assertion that *Babe Didrikson Zaharias, one of the most decorated female athletes of the twentieth century, is an inspiration for everyone*. The rest of the paragraph provides supporting details with facts showing why she is

an inspiration: the names of the illnesses she overcame, and the specific years she competed in the Olympics.

Be alert for **signal words**, which can be helpful in identifying supporting details. Signal words can also help you rule out sentences that are too broad to be the main idea or topic sentence: if a sentence begins with a signal word, it will likely be too specific to be a main idea.

Questions on the **CASA** will ask you to find details that support a particular idea and also to explain why a particular detail was included in the passage. In order to answer these questions, you must have a solid understanding of the passage's main idea. With this knowledge, you can determine how a supporting detail fits in with the larger structure of the passage.

Example

It's easy to puzzle over the landscapes of our solar system's distant planets—how could we ever know what those far-flung places really look like? However, scientists utilize a number of tools to visualize the surfaces of many planets. The topography of Venus, for example, has been explored by several space probes, including the Russian Venera landers and NASA's Magellan orbiter. These craft used imaging and radar to map the surface of the planet, identifying a whole host of features including volcanoes, craters, and a complex system of channels. Mars has likewise been mapped by space probes, including the famous Mars Rovers, which are automated vehicles that actually landed on the planet's surface. These rovers have been used by NASA and other space agencies to study the geology, climate, and possible biology of the planet.

In addition to these long-range probes, NASA has also used its series of orbiting telescopes to study distant planets. These four massively powerful telescopes include the famous Hubble Space Telescope as well as the Compton Gamma Ray Observatory, Chandra X-Ray Observatory, and the Spitzer Space Telescope. These allow scientists to examine planets using not only visible light but also infrared and near-infrared light, ultraviolet light, x-rays and gamma rays.

Powerful telescopes aren't just found in space: NASA makes use of Earth-bound telescopes as well. Scientists at the National Radio Astronomy Observatory in Charlottesville, VA, have spent decades using radio imaging to build an incredibly detailed portrait of Venus' surface. In fact, Earth-bound telescopes offer a distinct advantage over orbiting telescopes because they allow scientists to capture data from a fixed point, which in turn allows them to effectively compare data collected over long period of time.

Which sentence from the text best helps develop the idea that scientists make use of many different technologies to study the surfaces of other planets?

A)   *These rovers have been used by NASA and other space agencies to study the geology, climate, and possible biology of the planet.*

B)   *It's easy to puzzle over the landscapes of our solar system's distant planets—how could we ever know what those far-flung places really look like?*

C)   *In addition these long-range probes, NASA has also used its series of orbiting telescopes to study distant planets.*

D)   *These craft used imaging and radar to map the surface of the planet, identifying a whole host of features including volcanoes, craters, and a complex system of channels.*

You're looking for detail from the passage that supports the main idea—scientists make use of many different technologies to study the surfaces of other planets. Answer A) includes a specific detail about rovers, but does not offer any details that support the idea of multiple technologies being used. Similarly, answer D) provides another specific detail about space probes. Answer B) doesn't provide any supporting details; it simply introduces the topic of the passage. Only **answer C)** provides a detail that directly supports the author's assertion that scientists use multiple technologies to study the planets.

If true, which sentence could be added to the passage above to support the author's argument that scientists use many different technologies to study the surface of planets?

A)   *Because the Earth's atmosphere blocks x-rays, gamma rays, and infrared radiation, NASA needed to put telescopes in orbit above the atmosphere.*

B)   *In 2015, NASA released a map of Venus which was created by compiling images from orbiting telescopes and long-range space probes.*

C)   *NASA is currently using the Curiosity and Opportunity rovers to look for signs of ancient life on Mars.*

D)   *NASA has spent over $2.5 billion to build, launch, and repair the Hubble Space Telescope.*

You can eliminate answers C) and D) because they don't address the topic of studying the surface of planets. Answer A) can also be eliminated because it only addresses a single technology. Only **choice B)** would add support to the author's claim about the importance of using multiple technologies.

The author likely included the detail *Earth-bound telescopes offer a distinct advantage over orbiting telescopes because they allow scientists to capture data from a fixed point* in order to

A)   explain why it has taken scientists so long to map the surface of Venus.

B)   suggest that Earth-bound telescopes are the most important equipment used by NASA scientists.

C)   prove that orbiting telescopes will soon be replaced by Earth-bound telescopes.

D)   demonstrate why NASA scientists rely on many different types of scientific equipment.

Only **answer D)** relates directly to the author's main argument. The author doesn't mention how long it has taken to map the surface of Venus (answer A), nor does he say that one technology is more important than the others (answer B). And while this detail does highlight the advantages of using Earth-bound telescopes, the author's argument is that many technologies are being used at the same time, so there's no reason to think that orbiting telescopes will be replaced (answer C).

Understanding the Author

Author's Purpose

Whenever an author writes a text, she always has a purpose, whether that's to entertain, inform, explain, or persuade. A short story, for example, is meant to entertain, while an online news article would be designed to inform the public about a current event. Each of these different types of writing has a specific name:

- **Narrative** writing tells a story. (novel, short story, play)

- **Expository** writing informs people. (newspaper and magazine articles)

- **Technical** writing explains something. (product manual, directions)

- **Persuasive** writing tries to convince the reader of something. (opinion column on a blog)

On the exam, you may be asked to categorize a passage as one of these types, either by specifically naming it as such or by identifying its general purpose.

You may also be asked about primary and secondary sources. These terms describe not the writing itself but the author's relationship to what's being written about. A **primary source** is an unaltered piece of writing that was composed during the time when the events being described took place; these texts are often written by the people directly involved. A **secondary source** might address the same topic but provide extra commentary or analysis. These texts are written by outside observers and may even be composed after the event. For example, a book written by a political candidate to inform people about his or her stand on an issue is a primary source. An online article written by a journalist analyzing how that position will affect the election is a secondary source; a book by a historian about that election would be a secondary source, too.

Example

Elizabeth closed her eyes and braced herself on the armrests that divided her from her fellow passengers. Take-off was always the worst part for her. The revving of the engines, the way her stomach dropped as the plane lurched upward; it made her feel sick. Then, she had to watch the world fade away beneath her, getting smaller and smaller until it was just her and the clouds hurtling through the sky. Sometimes (but only sometimes) it just had to be endured, though. She focused on the thought of her sister's smiling face and her new baby nephew as the plane slowly pulled onto the runway.

The passage above is reflective of which type of writing?

A)   Narrative

B)   Expository

C)   Technical

D)   Persuasive

The passage is telling a story—we meet Elizabeth and learn about her fear of flying—so it's a narrative text, **answer choice A)**. There is no factual information presented or explained, nor is the author trying to persuade the reader of anything.

The Audience

A good author will write with a specific audience in mind. For example, an opinion column on a website might be specifically targeted toward undecided voters, or a brochure for an upcoming art exhibit might address people who have donated money to the museum in the past. The author's audience can influence what information is included in the text, the tone the author uses, and the structure of the text.

The easiest way to identify the intended audience of a text is simply to ask yourself who would benefit the most from the information in the passage. A passage about how often to change the oil in a car would provide useful information to new drivers, but likely wouldn't tell an experienced driver something she didn't already know. Thus, the audience is likely new drivers who are learning to take care of cars.

The author may also directly or indirectly refer to his audience. The author of an article on oil changes might say something like *new drivers will want to keep an eye on their mileage when deciding how often to get an oil change*, which tells the reader who the intended audience is.

Example

The museum's newest exhibit opens today! *The Ecology of the Columbia River Basin* is an exciting collaboration between the New Valley Museum of Natural Science and the U.S. Department of the Interior. The exhibit includes plants, insects, birds, and mammals that are unique to the Columbia River Basin and explores the changes that have occurred in this delicate ecosystem over the last century. The exhibit is kid friendly, with interactive, hands-on exhibits and exciting audio-visual presentations. Individual tickets are available on the museum's website, and groups may apply for special ticket prices by calling the museum directly.

The intended audience for this passage likely includes all of the following except

A)   a middle school biology teacher

B)   employees of the U.S. Department of the Interior

C)   parents of young children

D)   naturalists with an interest in local birds

The passage provides information to anyone who might be interested in an exhibit on the ecology of the Columbia River Basin. This includes biology teachers (who can get special group ticket prices), parents of young children (who now know the exhibit is kid friendly), and naturalists (who will want to see the unique birds). The only people who would not learn anything new from reading the passage are employees of the U.S. Department of the Interior **(answer B),** who likely already know about the exhibit since they helped create it.

Tone

The author of a text expresses how she feels about her subject and audience through the **tone** of the text. For example, a newspaper article about a prominent philanthropist might have be serious and appreciative, while a website blurb about an upcoming sale could be playful and relaxed.

Tone Words		
Positive	**Negative**	**Neutral**
admiring	angry	casual
approving	annoyed	detached
celebratory	belligerent	formal
comforting	bitter	impartial
confident	condescending	informal
earnest	confused	objective
encouraging	cynical	questioning
excited	depressed	unconcerned
forthright	derisive	
funny	despairing	
hopeful	disrespectful	
humorous	embarrassed	
modest	fearful	
nostalgic	gloomy	
optimistic	melancholy	
playful	mournful	
poignant	ominous	
proud	pessimistic	
relaxed	skeptical	
respectful	solemn	
sentimental	suspicious	
silly	unsympathetic	
sympathetic		

Authors signify tone in a number of ways. The main clue to look for is the author's **diction**, or word choice. Obviously, if the author is choosing words that have a negative connotation, then the overall tone of the text is negative, while words with a positive connotation will convey a positive tone. For example, the author of a biographical article may choose to describe his subject as *determined* or *pigheaded*; both mean similar things, but the first has a more positive connotation than the second. Literary devices such as imagery and metaphors can likewise generate a specific tone by evoking a particular feeling in the reader.

Tone is also developed by the structure of the text. Long, complicated sentences will make a passage seem formal, while short, pithy writing is more informal. Similarly, a text that cites statistical figures to support a logical argument will have a different tone that a text structured as a casual conversation between author and reader.

Example

It could be said that the great battle between the North and South we call the Civil War was a battle for individual identity. The states of the South had their own culture, one based on farming, independence, and the rights of both man and state to determine their own paths. Similarly, the North had forged its own identity as a center of centralized commerce and manufacturing. This clash of lifestyles was bound to create tension, and this tension was bound to lead to war. But people who try to sell you this narrative are wrong.

The tone of the passage above can best be described as

A)   formal and forthright

B)   casual and mournful

C)   detached and solemn

D)   objective and skeptical

The author of this passage is using a formal tone as indicated by his use of academic-sounding phrases like *rights of both man and state* and *centralized commerce*. He is also very forthright in his final sentence, when he directly and strongly states his opinion to the reader, so the **correct answer is A)**. Because of the formal language, the tone isn't *casual*, and the author's obvious strong feelings about the topic eliminate *detached* and *objective* as answer choices. The author's tone could be described as skeptical; however answer D) has already been eliminated.

Text Structure

Authors can structure passages in a number of different ways. These distinct organizational patterns, referred to as **text structure**, use the logical relationships between ideas to improve the readability and coherence of a text. The most common ways passages are organized include:

- **problem-solution**: the author presents a problem and then discusses a solution

- **comparison-contrast**: the author presents two situations and then discusses their similarities and differences

- **cause-effect**: the author presents an action and then discusses the resulting effects

- **descriptive**: the author describes an idea, object, person, or other item in detail

Example

The issue of public transportation has begun to haunt the fast-growing cities of the southern United States. Unlike their northern counterparts, cities like Atlanta, Dallas, and Houston have long promoted growth out and not up—these are cities full of sprawling suburbs and single-family homes, not densely concentrated skyscrapers and apartments. What to do then, when all those suburbanites need to get into the central business districts for work? For a long time it seemed highways were the twenty-lane wide expanses of concrete that would allow commuters to move from home to work and back again. But these modern miracles have become time-sucking, pollution-spewing nightmares. They may not like it, but it's time for these cities to turn toward public transport like trains and buses if they are to remain livable.

The organization of this passage can best be described as:

A)   a comparison of two similar ideas

B)   a description of a place

C)   a discussion of several effects all related to the same cause

D)   a discussion of a problem followed by the suggestion of a solution

You can exclude answer choice C) because the author provides no root cause or a list of effects. From there this question gets tricky, because the passage contains structures similar to those described above. For example, it compares two things (cities in the North and South) and describes a place (a sprawling city). However, if you look at the overall organization of the passage, you can see that it starts by presenting a problem (transportation) and then presents a solution (trains and buses), making **answer D)** the only choice that encompasses the entire passage.

Facts vs. Opinions

On the **CASA** you might be asked to identify a statement in a passage as either a fact or an opinion, so you'll need to know the difference between the two. A **fact** is a statement or thought that can be proven to be true. The statement *Wednesday comes after Tuesday* is a fact—you can point to a calendar to prove it. In contrast, an **opinion** is an assumption that is not based in fact and cannot be proven to be true. The assertion that *television is more entertaining than feature films* is an opinion—people will disagree on this, and there's no reference you can use to prove or disprove it.

Example

Exercise is critical for healthy development in children. Today, there is an epidemic of unhealthy children in the United States who will face health problems in adulthood due to poor diet and lack of exercise in childhood. This is a problem for all Americans, especially with the rising cost of healthcare.

It is vital that school systems and parents encourage their children to engage in a minimum of thirty minutes of cardiovascular exercise each day, mildly increasing their heart rate for a sustained period. This is proven to decrease the likelihood of developmental diabetes, obesity, and a multitude of other health problems. Also, children need a proper diet rich in fruits and vegetables so that they can grow and develop physically, as well as learn healthy eating habits early on.

Which of the following is a fact in the passage, not an opinion?

A)   Fruits and vegetables are the best way to help children be healthy.

B)   Children today are lazier than they were in previous generations.

C)   The risk of diabetes in children is reduced by physical activity.

D)   Children should engage in thirty minutes of exercise a day.

Answer: Choice B) can be discarded immediately because it is negative (recall that particularly negative answer statements are generally wrong) and is not discussed anywhere in the passage. Answers A) and D) are both opinions—the author is promoting exercise, fruits, and vegetables as a way to make children healthy. (Notice that these incorrect answers contain words that hint at being an opinion such as *best, should,* or other comparisons.) **Answer B)**, on the other hand, is a simple fact stated by the author; it appears in the passage with the word *proven,* indicating that you don't just need to take the author's word for it.

Drawing Conclusions

In addition to understanding the main idea and factual content of a passage, you'll also be asked to take your analysis one step further and anticipate what other information could logically be added to the passage. In a non-fiction passage, for example, you might be asked which statement the author of the passage would agree with. In an excerpt from a fictional work, you might be asked to anticipate what a character would do next.

To answer these questions, you must have a solid understanding of the topic, theme, and main idea of the passage; armed with this information, you can figure out which of the answer choices best fits within those criteria (or alternatively, which ones do not). For example, if the author of the passage is advocating for safer working conditions in textile factories, any supporting details that would be added to the passage should support that idea. You might add sentences that contain information about the number of accidents that occur in textile factories or that outline a new plan for fire safety. The key here is to pay very close attention to details: read critically and carefully.

Example

Today, there is an epidemic of unhealthy children in the United States who will face health problems in adulthood due to poor diet and lack of exercise during their childhoods. This is a problem for all Americans, as adults with chronic health issues are adding to the rising cost of healthcare. A child who grows up living an unhealthy lifestyle is likely to become an adult who does the same.

Because exercise is critical for healthy development in children, it is vital that school systems and parents encourage their children to engage in a minimum of thirty minutes of cardiovascular exercise each day. Even this small amount of exercise has been proven to decrease the likelihood that young people will develop diabetes, obesity, and other health issues as adults. In addition to exercise, children need a proper diet rich in fruits and vegetables so that they can grow and develop physically. Starting a good diet early also teaches children healthy eating habits they will carry into adulthood.

The author of this passage would most likely agree with which statement?

A)   Parents are solely responsible for the health of their children.

B)   Children who do not want to exercise should not be made to.

C)   Improved childhood nutrition will help lower the amount Americans spend on healthcare.

D)   It's not important to teach children healthy eating habits because they will learn them as adults.

The author would most likely support **answer C)**: he mentions in the first paragraph that poor diets are adding to the rising cost of healthcare. The main idea of the passage is that nutrition and exercise are important for children, so answer B) doesn't make sense—the author would likely support measures to encourage children to exercise. Answers A) and D) can also be eliminated because they are directly contradicted in the text. The author specifically mentions the role of school systems, so he doesn't believe parents are solely responsible for their children's health. He also specifically states that children who grow up with unhealthy eating habits will become adults with unhealthy eating habits, which contradicts D).

Elizabeth closed her eyes and braced herself on the armrests that divided her from her fellow passengers. Take-off was always the worst part for her. The revving of the engines, the way her stomach dropped as the plane lurched upward; it made her feel sick. Then, she had to watch the world fade away beneath her, getting smaller and smaller until it was just her and the clouds hurtling through the sky. Sometimes (but only sometimes) it just had to be endured, though. She focused on the thought of her sister's smiling face and her new baby nephew as the plane slowly pulled onto the runway.

Which of the following is Elizabeth least likely to do in the future?

A)   Take a flight to her brother's wedding.

B)   Apply for a job as a flight attendant.

C)   Never board an airplane again.

D)   Get sick on an airplane.

It's clear from the passage that Elizabeth hates flying, but it willing to endure it for the sake of visiting her family. Thus, it seems likely that she would be willing to get on a plane for her brother's wedding, making A) and C) incorrect answers. The passage also explicitly tells us that she feels sick on planes, so D) is likely to happen. We can infer, though, that she would not enjoy being on an airplane for work, so she's very unlikely to apply for a job as a flight attendant, which is **choice B)**.

Meaning of Words and Phrases

On the Reading section you may be asked to provide definitions or intended meanings for words within passages. You may have never encountered some of these words before the test, but there are tricks you can use to figure out what they mean.

Context Clues

A fundamental vocabulary skill is using context to determine the meaning of a word. There are two types of context that can help you understand unfamiliar words: situational context and sentence context. Regardless of which context you encounter, these types of questions are not really testing your knowledge of vocabulary; rather, they test your ability to comprehend the meaning of a word through its usage.

Situational context helps you determine the meaning of a word through the setting or circumstances in which that word or phrase occurs. Using **sentence context** requires analyzing only the sentence in which the new word appears to understand it. To figure out words using sentence context clues, you should first identify the most important words in the sentence.

There are four types of clues that can help you understand the context, and therefore the meaning of a word:

- **Restatement** clues occur when the definition of the word is clearly stated in the sentence.
- **Positive/negative clues** can tell you whether a word has a positive or negative meaning.
- **Contrast clues** include the opposite meaning of a word. Words like *but*, *on the other hand*, and *however* are tip-offs that a sentence contains a contrast clue.
- **Specific detail clues** provide a precise detail that can help you understand the meaning of the word.

It is important to remember that more than one of these clues can be present in the same sentence. The more there are, the easier it will be to determine the meaning of the word. For example, the following sentence uses both restatement and positive/negative clues: *Janet suddenly found herself destitute, so poor she could barely afford to eat*. The second part of the sentence clearly indicates that *destitute* is a negative word. It also restates the meaning: very poor.

Examples

I had a hard time reading her *illegible* handwriting.

A)   neat

B)   unsafe

C)   sloppy

D)   educated

Already, you know that this sentence is discussing something that is hard to read. Look at the word that *illegible* is describing: handwriting. Based on context clues, you can tell that *illegible* means that her handwriting is hard to read.

Next, look at the answer choices. Choice A), *neat,* is obviously a wrong answer because neat handwriting would not be difficult to read. Choices B) and D), *unsafe* and *educated,* don't make sense. Therefore, **choice C)**, *sloppy,* is the best answer.

The dog was *dauntless* in the face of danger, braving the fire to save the girl trapped inside the building.

A)   difficult

B)   fearless

C)   imaginative

D)   startled

Demonstrating bravery in the face of danger would be **B), *fearless***. In this case, the restatement clue (*braving the fire*) tells you exactly what the word means.

Beth did not spend any time preparing for the test, but Tyrone kept a *rigorous* study schedule.

A)   strict

B)   loose

C)   boring

D)   strange

In this case, the contrast word *but* tells us that Tyrone studied in a different way than Beth, which means it's a contrast clue. If Beth did not study hard, then Tyrone did. The best answer, therefore, is choice A).

Analyzing Words

As you no doubt know, determining the meaning of a word can be more complicated than just looking in a dictionary. A word might have more than one **denotation**, or definition; which one the author intends can only be judged by examining the surrounding text. For example, the word *quack* can refer to the sound a duck makes, or to a person who publicly pretends to have a qualification which he or she does not actually possess.

A word may also have different **connotations**, which are the implied meanings and emotions a word evokes in the reader. For example, a cubicle is a simply a walled desk in an office, but for many the word implies a constrictive, uninspiring workplace. Connotations can vary greatly between cultures and even between individuals.

Lastly, authors might make use of **figurative language**, which is the use of a word to imply something other than the word's literal definition. This is often done by comparing two things. If you say *I felt like a butterfly when I got a new haircut*, the listener knows you don't resemble an insect but instead felt beautiful and transformed.

Word Structure

Although you are not expected to know every word in the English language for the **CASA**, you can use deductive reasoning to determine the answer choice that is the best match for the word in question by breaking down unfamiliar vocabulary. Many complex words can be broken down into three main parts:

prefix – root – suffix

Roots are the building blocks of all words. Every word is either a root itself or has a root. Just as a plant cannot grow without roots, neither can vocabulary, because a word must have a root to give it meaning. The root is what is left when you strip away all the prefixes and suffixes from a word. For example, in the word *unclear*, if you take away the prefix *un-*, you have the root *clear*.

Roots are not always recognizable words; they generally come from Latin or Greek words like *nat*, a Latin root meaning *born*. The word *native*, which describes a person born in a referenced place, comes from this root, as does the word *prenatal*, meaning *before birth*. It's important to keep in mind, however, that roots do not always match the exact definitions of words, and they can have several different spellings.

Prefixes are syllables added to the beginning of a word, and **suffixes** are syllables added to the end of the word. Both carry assigned meanings and can be attached to a word to completely change the word's meaning or to enhance the word's original meaning.

Take the word *prefix* itself as an example: *fix* means to place something securely and *pre-* means before. Therefore, *prefix* means *to place something before* or *in front of*. Now let's look at a suffix: in the word *portable*, *port* is a root which means to *move* or *carry*. The suffix *-able* means that something is possible. Thus, *portable* describes something that can be moved or carried.

Although you cannot determine the meaning of a word by a prefix or suffix alone, you can use this knowledge to eliminate answer choices; understanding whether the word is positive or negative can give you the partial meaning of the word.

Comparing Passages

In addition to analyzing single passages, the **CASA** will also require you to compare two passages. Usually these passages will discuss the same topic, and it will be your task to identify the similarities and differences between the authors' main ideas, supporting details, and tones.

Examples

Read the two passages below and answer the following questions.

Passage 1

Today, there is an epidemic of unhealthy children in the United States who will face health problems in adulthood due to poor diet and lack of exercise during their childhoods: in 2012, the Centers for Disease Control found that 18 percent of students aged 6-11 were obese. This is a problem for all Americans, as adults with chronic health issues are adding to the rising cost of healthcare. A child who grows up living an unhealthy lifestyle is likely to become an adult who does the same.

Because exercise is critical for healthy development in children, it is vital that school systems and parents encourage their children to engage in a minimum of thirty minutes of cardiovascular exercise each day. Even this small amount of exercise has been proven to decrease the likelihood that young people will develop diabetes, obesity, and other health issues as adults. In addition to exercise, children need a proper diet rich in fruits and vegetables so that they can grow and develop physically. Starting a good diet early also teaches children healthy eating habits they will carry into adulthood.

Passage 2

When was the last time you took a good, hard look at a school lunch? For many adults, it's probably been years—decades even—since they last thought about students' midday meals. If they did stop to ponder, they might picture something reasonably wholesome if not very exciting: a peanut butter and jelly sandwich paired with an apple, or a traditional plate of meat, potatoes and veggies. At worst, they may think, kids are making due with some pizza and a carton of milk.

The truth, though, is that many students aren't even getting the meager nutrients offered up by a simple slice of pizza. Instead, schools are serving up heaping helpings of previously frozen, recently fried delicacies like french fries and chicken nuggets. These high-carb, low-protein options are usually paired with a limp, flavorless, straight-from-the-freezer vegetable that quickly gets tossed in the trash. And that carton of milk? It's probably a sugar-filled chocolate sludge, or it's been replaced with a student's favorite high-calorie soda.

So what, you might ask. Kids like to eat junk food—it's a habit they'll grow out of soon enough. Besides, parents can always pack lunches for students looking for something better. But is that really the lesson we want to be teaching our kids? Many of those children aren't going to grow out of bad habits; they're going to reach adulthood thinking that ketchup is a vegetable. And students in low-income families are particularly impacted by the sad state of school food. These parents rely on schools to provide a warm, nutritious meal because they don't have the time or money to prepare food at home. Do we really want to be punishing these children with soggy meat patties and salt-soaked potato chips?

Both authors are arguing for the important of improving childhood nutrition. How do the authors' strategies differ?

A)   Passage 1 presents several competing viewpoints while Passage 2 offers a single argument.

B)   Passage 1 uses scientific data while Passage 2 uses figurative language.

C)   Passage 1 is descriptive while Passage 2 uses a cause-effect structure.

D)   Passage 1 has a friendly tone while the tone of Passage 2 is angry.

The first author uses scientific facts (*the Centers for Disease Control found* . . . and *Even this small amount of exercise has been proven* . . .) to back up his argument, while the second uses figurative language (the ironic *delicacies* and the metaphor *sugar-filled chocolate sludge*), so the **correct answer is B)**. Answer A) is incorrect because the first author does present any opposing viewpoints. Answer C) is incorrect because Passage 2 does not have a cause-effect structure.

And while the author of the second passage could be described as angry, the first author is not particularly friendly, so you can eliminate answer D) as well.

Both authors argue that

A)   children should learn healthy eating habits at a young age.

B)   low-income students are disproportionately affected by the low-quality food offered in schools.

C)   teaching children about good nutrition will lower their chances of developing diabetes as adults.

D)   schools should provide children an opportunity to exercise every day.

Both authors argue children should learn healthy eating habits at a young age **(answer A)**. The author of Passage 1 states that *a child who grows up living an unhealthy lifestyle is likely to become an adult who does the same*, and the author of Passage 2 states that *many of those children aren't going to grow out of bad habits*—both of these sentences argue that it's necessary to teach children about nutrition early in life. Answers C) and D) are mentioned only by the author of Passage 1, and answer B) is only discussed in Passage 2.

Chapter 2: Mathematics

The **CASA** Mathematics section covers high-school level topics including basic operations, algebra, geometry, statistics, and probability. Most questions will cover algebraic topics, including setting up and solving a variety of equations and inequalities; you'll likely see only a few questions on statistics and probability. The section includes 40 multiple-choice questions and 12 gridded-response questions.

Strategies for the Mathematics Section

Go Back to the Basics

First and foremost, practice your basic skills: sign changes, order of operations, simplifying fractions, and equation manipulation. These are the skills used most on the **CASA**, though they are applied in different contexts. Remember that when it comes down to it, all math problems rely on the four basic skills of addition, subtraction, multiplication, and division. All you need to figure out is the order in which they're used to solve a problem.

Don't Rely on Mental Math

Using mental math is great for eliminating answer choices, but ALWAYS WRITE DOWN YOUR WORK! This cannot be stressed enough. Use whatever paper is provided; by writing and/or drawing out the problem, you are more likely to catch any mistakes. The act of writing things down also forces you to organize your calculations, leading to an improvement in your **CASA** score.

The Three-Times Rule

You should read each question at least three times to ensure you're using the correct information and answering the right question:

Step One: Read the question and write out the given information.

Step Two: Read the question, set up your equation(s), and solve.

Step Three: Read the question and check that your answer makes sense (is the amount too large or small; is the answer in the correct unit of measurement, etc.).

Make an Educated Guess

Eliminate those answer choices which you are relatively sure are incorrect, and then guess from the remaining choices. Educated guessing is critical to increasing your score.

Numbers and Operations

In order to do any type of math—whether it's basic geometry or advanced calculus—you need to have a solid understanding of numbers and operations. The specific operations the **CASA** will test you on are covered in this chapter. However, we won't be covering basic arithmetic operations like adding fractions or long division, since you'll be able to perform these on your calculator during the test.

Types of Numbers

Integers are whole numbers, including the counting numbers, the negative counting numbers and zero. 3, 2, 1, 0, -1, -2, -3 are examples of integers. **Rational numbers** are made by dividing one integer by another integer. They can be expressed as fractions or as decimals. 3 divided by 4 makes the rational number ¾ or 0.75. **Irrational numbers** are numbers that cannot be written as fractions; they are decimals that go on forever without repeating. The number π (3.14159...) is an example of an irrational number.

Imaginary numbers are numbers that, when squared, give a negative result. Imaginary numbers use the symbol i to represent $\sqrt{-1}$, so $3i = 3\sqrt{-1}$ and $(3i)^2 = -9$. **Complex numbers** are combinations of real and imaginary numbers, written in the form $a + bi$, where a is the real number and b is the imaginary number. An example of a complex number is 4 + 2i. When adding complex numbers, add the real and imaginary numbers separately: $(4 + 2i) + (3 + i) = 7 + 3i$.

Examples

Is $\sqrt{5}$ a rational or irrational number?

Answer:

$\sqrt{5}$ is an **irrational number** because it cannot be written as a fraction of two integers. It is a decimal that goes on forever without repeating.

What kind of number is $-\sqrt{64}$?

Answer:

$-\sqrt{64}$ can be rewritten as the negative whole number -8, so it is an **integer**.

Solve $(3 + 5i) - (1 - 2i)$

Answer:

Subtract the real and imaginary numbers separately.

$3 - 1 = 2$

$5i - (-2i) = 5i + 2i = 7i$

So $(3 + 5i) - (1 - 2i) = \mathbf{2 + 7i}$

Roman Numerals

The Roman numeral system uses letters to represent numerical values, as shown below.

Roman Numeral	Value
I	1
V	5
X	10
L	50
C	100
D	500
M	1000

These seven numerals are combined to form numbers. Numerals are always arranged from greatest to least in value starting with the largest possible number. For example, the number 157 would be written as 100 + 50 + 5 + 1 + 1 = CLVII, and the number 3,621 is written as 1000 + 1000 + 1000 + 500 + 100 + 10 + 10 + 1 = MMMDCXXI.

To avoid adding four of the same numerals in a row, subtraction is used. If a numeral with a smaller value is placed before a numeral with a larger value, the smaller number is subtracted from the bigger number. For example, the number 9 is written as IX (10 − 1 = 9). Since I has a value of 1 and it is placed before X, which has a value of 10, the number is found by subtracting 1 from 10.

Examples

Express the number 538 in Roman numerals.

Answer:

538 = 500 + 30 + 8

538 = 500 + 10 + 10 + 10 + 5 + 1 + 1 + 1

538 = **DXXXVIII**

What number is expressed by the Roman numeral CDVII?

Answer:

C = 100, D = 500, V = 5, I = 1, I = 1

Since C comes before D, 100 is subtracted from 500.

500 − 100 + 5 + 1 + 1 = **407**

Working with Positive and Negative Numbers

Adding, multiplying, and dividing numbers can yield positive or negative values depending on the signs of the original numbers. Knowing these rules can help determine if your answer is correct.

(+) + (−) = the sign of the larger number

(−) + (−) = negative number

(−) × (−) = positive number

(−) × (+) = negative number

(−) ÷ (−) = positive number

(−) ÷ (+) = negative number

Examples

Find the product of −10 and 47.

    Answer:

    (−) × (+) = (−)

    −10 × 47 = **−470**

What is the sum of −65 and −32?

    Answer:

    (−) + (−) = (−)

    −65 + −32 = **−97**

Is the product of −7 and 4 less than −7, between −7 and 4, or greater than 4?

    Answer:

    (−) × (+) = (−)

    −7 × 4 = −28, which is **less than −7**

What is the value of −16 divided by 2.5?

    Answer:

    (−) ÷ (+) = (−)

    −16 ÷ 2.5 = **−6.4**

Order of Operations

Operations in a mathematical expression are always performed in a specific order, which is described by the acronym PEMDAS:

1. Parentheses

2. Exponents

3. Multiplication

4. Division

5. Addition

6. Subtraction

Perform the operations within parentheses first, and then address any exponents. After those steps, perform all multiplication and division. These are carried out from left to right as they appear in the problem. Finally, do all required addition and subtraction, also from left to right as each operation appears in the problem.

Examples

Solve [–(2)² – (4 + 7)]

> Answer:
>
> First, complete operations within parentheses:
>
> $-(2)^2 - (11)$
>
> Second, calculate the value of exponential numbers:
>
> $-(4) - (11)$
>
> Finally, do addition and subtraction:
>
> $-4 - 11 = -15$

Solve $(5)^2 \div 5 + 4 \times 2$

Answer:

First, calculate the value of exponential numbers:

$(25) \div 5 + 4 \times 2$

Second, calculate division and multiplication from left to right:

$5 + 8$

Finally, do addition and subtraction:

$5 + 8 = \mathbf{13}$

Solve the expression $15 \times (4 + 8) - 3^3$

Answer:

First, complete operations within parentheses:

$15 \times (12) - 3^3$

Second, calculate the value of exponential numbers:

$15 \times (12) - 27$

Third, calculate division and multiplication from left to right:

$180 - 27$

Finally, do addition and subtraction from left to right:

$180 - 27 = \mathbf{153}$

Solve the expression $(\frac{5}{2} \times 4) + 23 - 4^2$

Answer:

First, complete operations within parentheses:

$(10) + 23 - 4^2$

Second, calculate the value of exponential numbers:

$(10) + 23 - 16$

Finally, do addition and subtraction from left to right:

$(10) + 23 - 16$

$33 - 16 = \mathbf{17}$

Units of Measurement

You are expected to memorize some units of measurement. These are given below. When doing unit conversion problems (i.e., when converting one unit to another), find the conversion factor, then apply that factor to the given measurement to find the new units.

PREFIX	SYMBOL	MULTIPLICATION FACTOR
tera	T	1,000,000,000,000
giga	G	1,000,000,000
mega	M	1,000,000
kilo	k	1,000
hecto	h	100
deca	da	10
base unit	--	--
deci	d	0.1
centi	c	0.01
milli	m	0.001
micro	μ	0.0000001
nano	n	0.0000000001
pico	p	0.0000000000001

DIMENSION	AMERICAN	SI
length	inch/foot/yard/mile	meter
mass	ounce/pound/ton	gram
volume	cup/pint/quart/gallon	liter
force	pound-force	newton
pressure	pound-force per square inch	pascal
work and energy	cal/British thermal unit	joule
temperature	Fahrenheit	kelvin
charge	faraday	coulomb

Examples

A fence measures 15 ft. long. How many yards long is the fence?

Answer:

1 yd. = 3 ft.

$\frac{15}{3}$ = **5 yd.**

A pitcher can hold 24 cups. How many gallons can it hold?

Answer:

1 gal. = 16 cups

$\frac{24}{16}$ = **1.5 gal.**

A spool of wire holds 144 in. of wire. If Mario has 3 spools, how many feet of wire does he have?

Answer:

12 in. = 1 ft.

$\frac{144}{12}$ = 12 ft.

12 ft. × 3 spools = **36 ft. of wire**

A ball rolling across a table travels 6 inches per second. How many feet will it travel in 1 minute?

Answer:

This problem can be worked in two steps: finding how many inches are covered in 1 minute, and then converting that value to feet. It can also be worked the opposite way, by finding how many feet it travels in 1 second and then converting that to feet traveled per minute. The first method is shown below.

1 min. = 60 sec.

$\frac{6 \text{ in.}}{\text{sec.}}$ × 60 s = 360 in.

1 ft. = 12 in.

$$\frac{360 \text{ in.}}{12 \text{ in.}} = \textbf{30 ft.}$$

How many millimeters are in 0.5 meters?

Answer:

1 meter = 1000 mm

0.5 meters = **500 mm**

A lead ball weighs 38 g. How many kilograms does it weigh?

Answer:

1 kg = 1000 g

$$\frac{38 \text{ g}}{1000 \text{ g}} = \textbf{0.038 kg}$$

How many cubic centimeters are in 10 L?

Answer:

1 L = 1000 cm^3

10 L = 1000 cm^3 × 10

10 L = **10,000 cm^3**

Jennifer's pencil was initially 10 centimeters long. After she sharpened it, it was 9.6 centimeters long. How many millimeters did she lose from her pencil by sharpening it?

Answer:

1 cm = 10 mm

10 cm − 9.6 cm = 0.4 cm lost

0.4 cm = 10 × 0.4 mm = **4 mm were lost**

Decimals and Fractions

Adding and Subtracting Decimals

When adding and subtracting decimals, line up the numbers so that the decimals are aligned. You want to subtract the ones place from the ones place, the tenths place from the tenths place, etc.

Examples

Find the sum of 17.07 and 2.52.

Answer:

17.07

+ 2.52

= 19.59

Jeannette has 7.4 gallons of gas in her tank. After driving, she has 6.8 gallons. How many gallons of gas did she use?

Answer:

7.4

− 6.8

= 0.6 gal.

Multiplying and Dividing Decimals

When multiplying decimals, start by multiplying the numbers normally. You can then determine the placement of the decimal point in the result by adding the number of digits after the decimal in each of the numbers you multiplied together.

When dividing decimals, you should move the decimal point in the divisor (the number you're dividing by) until it is a whole. You can then move the decimal in the dividend (the number you're dividing into) the same number of places in the same direction. Finally, divide the new numbers normally to get the correct answer.

Example

What is the product of 0.25 and 1.4?

> Answer:
>
> $25 \times 14 = \textbf{350}$
>
> There are 2 digits after the decimal in 0.25 and one digit after the decimal in 1.4. Therefore the product should have 3 digits after the decimal: **0.350** is the correct answer.

Find $0.8 \div 0.2$.

> Answer:
>
> Change 0.2 to 2 by moving the decimal one space to the right.
>
> Next, move the decimal one space to the right on the dividend. 0.8 becomes 8.
>
> Now, divide 8 by 2. $8 \div 2 = \textbf{4}$

Find the quotient when 40 is divided by 0.25.

> Answer:
>
> First, change the divisor to a whole number: 0.25 becomes 25.
>
> Next, change the dividend to match the divisor by moving the decimal two spaces to the right, so 40 becomes 4000.
>
> Now divide: $4000 \div 25 = \textbf{160}$

Working with Fractions

Fractions are made up of two parts: the **numerator**, which appears above the bar, and the **denominator**, which is below it. If a fraction is in its **simplest form**, the numerator and the denominator share no common factors. A fraction with a numerator larger than its denominator is an **improper fraction**; when the denominator is larger, it's a **proper fraction**.

Improper fractions can be converted into proper fractions by dividing the numerator by the denominator. The resulting whole number is placed to the left of the fraction, and the remainder becomes the new numerator; the denominator does not change. The new number is called a **mixed number** because it contains a whole number and a fraction. Mixed numbers can be turned into improper fractions through the reverse process: multiply the whole number by the denominator and add the numerator to get the new numerator.

Examples

Simplify the fraction $\frac{121}{77}$.

Answer:

121 and 77 share a common factor of 11. So, if we divide each by 11 we can simplify the fraction:

$$\frac{121}{77} = \frac{11}{11} \times \frac{11}{7} = \mathbf{\frac{11}{7}}$$

Convert $\frac{37}{5}$ into a proper fraction.

Answer:

Start by dividing the numerator by the denominator:

$37 \div 5 = 7$ with a remainder of 2

Now build a mixed number with the whole number and the new numerator:

$$\frac{37}{5} = \mathbf{7\frac{2}{5}}$$

Multiplying and Dividing Fractions

To multiply fractions, convert any mixed numbers into improper fractions and multiply the numerators together and the denominators together. Reduce to lowest terms if needed.

To divide fractions, first convert any mixed fractions into single fractions. Then, invert the second fraction so that the denominator and numerator are switched. Finally, multiply the numerators together and the denominators together.

Examples

What is the product of $\frac{1}{12}$ and $\frac{6}{8}$?

This is a fraction multiplication problem, so simply multiply the numerators together and the denominators together and then reduce:

$$\frac{1}{12} \times \frac{6}{8} = \frac{6}{96} = \frac{1}{16}$$

Sometimes it's easier to reduce fractions before multiplying if you can:

$$\frac{1}{12} \times \frac{6}{8} = \frac{1}{12} \times \frac{3}{4} = \frac{3}{48} = \frac{1}{16}$$

Find $\frac{7}{8} \div \frac{1}{4}$.

For a fraction division problem, invert the second fraction and then multiply and reduce:

$$\frac{7}{8} \div \frac{1}{4} = \frac{7}{8} \times \frac{4}{1} = \frac{28}{8} = \frac{7}{2}$$

What is the quotient of $\frac{2}{5} \div 1\frac{1}{5}$?

Answer:

This is a fraction division problem, so the first step is to convert the mixed number to an improper fraction:

$$1\frac{1}{5} = \frac{5 \times 1}{5} + \frac{1}{5} = \frac{6}{5}$$

Now, divide the fractions. Remember to invert the second fraction, and then multiply normally:

$$\frac{2}{5} \div \frac{6}{5} = \frac{2}{5} \times \frac{5}{6} = \frac{10}{30} = \frac{1}{3}$$

A recipe calls for $\frac{1}{4}$ cup of sugar. If 8.5 batches of the recipe are needed, how many cups of sugar will be used?

Answer:

This is a fraction multiplication problem: $\frac{1}{4} \times 8\frac{1}{2}$.

First, we need to convert the mixed number into a proper fraction:

$$8\frac{1}{2} = \frac{8 \times 2}{2} + \frac{1}{2} = \frac{17}{2}$$

Now, multiply the fractions across the numerators and denominators, and then reduce:

$$\frac{1}{4} \times 8\frac{1}{2} = \frac{1}{4} \times \frac{17}{2} = \frac{17}{8} \text{ cups of sugar}$$

Adding and Subtracting Fractions

Adding and subtracting fractions requires a **common denominator**. To find the common denominator, you can multiply each fraction by the number 1. With fractions, any number over itself (e.g., $\frac{5}{5}, \frac{12}{12}$, etc.) is equivalent to 1, so multiplying by such a fraction can change the denominator without changing the value of the fraction. Once the denominators are the same, the numerators can be added or subtracted.

To add mixed numbers, you can first add the whole numbers and then the fractions. To subtract mixed numbers, convert each number to an improper fraction, then subtract the numerators.

Examples

Simplify the expression $\frac{2}{3} - \frac{1}{5}$.

Answer:

First, multiply each fraction by a factor of 1 to get a common denominator. How do you know which factor of 1 to use? Look at the other fraction and use the number found in that denominator:

$$\frac{2}{3} - \frac{1}{5} = \frac{2}{3}\left(\frac{5}{5}\right) - \frac{1}{5}\left(\frac{3}{3}\right) = \frac{10}{15} - \frac{3}{15}$$

Once the fractions have a common denominator, simply subtract the numerators:

$$\frac{10}{15} - \frac{3}{15} = \frac{7}{15}$$

Find $2\frac{1}{3} - \frac{3}{2}$.

Answer:

This is a fraction subtraction problem with a mixed number, so the first step is to convert the mixed number to an improper fraction:

$$2\frac{1}{3} = \frac{2\times3}{3} + \frac{1}{3} = \frac{7}{3}$$

Next, convert each fraction so they share a common denominator:

$$\frac{7}{3} \times \frac{2}{2} = \frac{14}{6}$$

$$\frac{3}{2} \times \frac{3}{3} = \frac{9}{6}$$

Now, subtract the fractions by subtracting the numerators:

$$\frac{14}{6} - \frac{9}{6} = \frac{5}{6}$$

Find the sum of $\frac{9}{16}$, $\frac{1}{2}$, and $\frac{7}{4}$.

Answer:

For this fraction addition problem, we need to find a common denominator. Notice that 2 and 4 are both factors of 16, so 16 can be the common denominator:

$$\frac{1}{2} \times \frac{8}{8} = \frac{8}{16}$$

$$\frac{7}{4} \times \frac{4}{4} = \frac{28}{16}$$

$$\frac{9}{16} + \frac{8}{16} + \frac{28}{16} = \mathbf{\frac{45}{16}}$$

Sabrina has $\frac{2}{3}$ of a can of red paint. Her friend Amos has $\frac{1}{6}$ of a can. How much red paint do they have combined?

Answer:

To add fractions, make sure that they have a common denominator. Since 3 is a factor of 6, 6 can be the common denominator:

$$\frac{2}{3} \times \frac{2}{2} = \frac{4}{6}$$

Now, add the numerators:

$$\frac{4}{6} + \frac{1}{6} = \frac{5}{6} \textbf{ of a can}$$

Converting Fractions to Decimals

Calculators are not allowed on the **CASA**, which can make handling fractions and decimals intimidating for many test-takers. However, there are several helpful techniques you can use to navigate between the two forms.

The first thing to do is simply memorize common decimals and their fractional equivalents; a list of these is given below. With these values, it's possible to convert more complicated fractions as well. For example, $\frac{2}{5}$ is just $\frac{1}{5}$ multiplied by 2, so $\frac{2}{5} = 0.2 \times 2 = 0.4$.

fraction	decimal
$\frac{1}{2}$	0.5
$\frac{1}{3}$	$0.\overline{33}$
$\frac{1}{4}$	0.25
$\frac{1}{5}$	0.2
$\frac{1}{6}$	$0.1\overline{66}$
$\frac{1}{7}$	$0.\overline{142857}$
$\frac{1}{8}$	0.125
$\frac{1}{9}$	$0.\overline{11}$
$\frac{1}{10}$	0.1

Knowledge of common decimal equivalents to fractions can also help you estimate. This skill can be particularly helpful on multiple-choice tests like the **CASA**, where excluding incorrect answers can be just as helpful as knowing how to find the right one. For example, to find $\frac{5}{8}$ in decimal form for an answer, you can eliminate any answers less than 0.5 because $\frac{4}{8} = 0.5$. You may also know that $\frac{6}{8}$ is the same as ¾ or 0.75, so anything above 0.75 can be eliminated as well.

Another helpful trick is to check if the denominator is easily divisible by 100; for example in the fraction $\frac{9}{20}$, you know 20 goes into 100 five times, so you can multiply the top and bottom by 5 to get $\frac{45}{100}$ or 0.45.

If none of these techniques work, you'll need to find the decimal by dividing the denominator by the numerator using long division.

Examples

Write $\frac{8}{18}$ as a decimal.

Answer:

The first step here is to simplify the fraction:

$$\frac{8}{18} = \frac{4}{9}$$

Now it's clear that the fraction is a multiple of $\frac{1}{9}$, so you can easily find the decimal using a value you already know:

$$\frac{4}{9} = \frac{1}{9} \times 4 = 0.\overline{11} \times 4 = \mathbf{0.\overline{44}}$$

Write the fraction $\frac{3}{16}$ as a decimal.

Answer:

None of the tricks above will work for this fraction, so you need to do long division:

$$\begin{array}{r} 1875 \\ \overline{16\smash{)}\,3.0} \\ 14.0 \\ \overline{12} \\ \overline{8.0} \end{array}$$

The decimal will go in front of the answer, so now you know that $\frac{3}{16} = \mathbf{0.1875}$.

Converting Decimals to Fractions

Converting a decimal into a fraction is more straightforward than the reverse process is. To convert a decimal, simply use the numbers that come after the decimal as the numerator in the fraction. The denominator will be a power of 10 that matches the place value for the original decimal. For example, the numerator for 0.46 would be 100 because the last number is in the tenths place; likewise, the denominator for 0.657 would be 1000 because the last number is in the thousandths place. Once this fraction has been set up, all that's left is to simplify it.

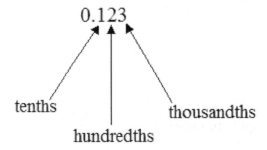

Example

Convert 0.45 into a fraction.

> The last number in the decimal is in the hundredths place, so we can easily set up a fraction:
>
> $$0.45 = \frac{45}{100}$$
>
> The next step is simply to reduce the fraction down to the lowest common denominator. Here, both 45 and 100 are divisible by 5. 45 divided by 5 is 9, and 100 divided by 5 is 20. Therefore, you're left with:
>
> $$\frac{45}{100} = \frac{9}{20}$$

Ratios

A **ratio** describes the quantity of one thing in relation to the quantity of another. Unlike fractions, ratios do not give a part relative to a whole; instead, they compare two values. For example, if you have 3 apples and 4 oranges, the ratio of apples to oranges is 3 to 4. Ratios can be written using words (3 to 4), fractions ($\frac{3}{4}$), or colons (3:4).

It's helpful to rewrite a ratio as a fraction expressing a part to a whole. For instance, in the example above you have 7 total pieces of fruit, so the fraction of your fruit that is apples is $\frac{3}{7}$, while oranges make up $\frac{4}{7}$ of your fruit collection.

When working with ratios, always consider the units of the values being compared. On the **CASA**, you may be asked to rewrite a ratio using the same units on both sides. For example, you might have to rewrite the ratio 3 minutes to 7 seconds as 180 seconds to 7 seconds.

Examples

There are 90 voters in a room, and each is either a Democrat or a Republican. The ratio of Democrats to Republicans is 5:4. How many Republicans are there?

Answer:

We know that there are 5 Democrats for every 4 Republicans in the room, which means for every 9 people, 4 are Republicans.

$5 + 4 = 9$

Fraction of Democrats: $\frac{5}{9}$

Fraction of Republicans: $\frac{4}{9}$

If $\frac{4}{9}$ of the 90 voters are Republicans, then:

$\frac{4}{9} \times 90 =$ **40 voters are Republicans**

The ratio of students to teachers in a school is 15:1. If there are 38 teachers, how many students attend the school?

Answer:

To solve this ratio problem, we can simply multiply both sides of the ratio by the desired value to find the number of students that correspond to having 38 teachers:

$$\frac{15 \text{ students}}{1 \text{ teacher}} \times \frac{38}{38} = \frac{570 \text{ students}}{38 \text{ teachers}}$$

The school has **570 students**.

Proportions

A **proportion** is an equation which states that 2 ratios are equal. Proportions are usually written as 2 fractions joined by an equal sign ($\frac{a}{b} = \frac{c}{d}$), but they can also be written using colons (a : b :: c : d). Note that in a proportion, the units must be the same in both numerators and in both denominators.

Often you will be given 3 of the values in a proportion and asked to find the 4th. In these types of problems, you can solve for the missing variable by cross-multiplying—multiply the numerator of each fraction by the denominator of the other to get an equation with no fractions as shown below. You can then solve the equation using basic algebra. (For more on solving basic equations, see "Algebraic Expressions and Equations").

$$\frac{a}{b} = \frac{c}{d} \rightarrow ad = bc$$

Examples

A train traveling 120 miles takes 3 hours to get to its destination. How long will it take for the train to travel 180 miles?

Answer:

Start by setting up the proportion:

$$\frac{120 \text{ mi}}{3 \text{ hrs}} = \frac{180 \text{ mi}}{x \text{ hr}}$$

Note that it doesn't matter which value is placed in the numerator or denominator, as long as it is the same on both sides. Now, solve for the missing quantity through cross-multiplication:

$$120 \text{ mi} \times x \text{ hr} = 3 \text{ hrs} \times 180 \text{ mi}$$

Now solve the equation:

$$x \text{ hours} = \frac{(3 \text{ hrs}) \times (180 \text{ mi})}{120 \text{ mi}}$$

x = 4.5 hrs

One acre of wheat requires 500 gallons of water. How many acres can be watered with 2600 gallons?

Answer:

Set up the equation:

$$\frac{1 \text{ acre}}{500 \text{ gal}} = \frac{x \text{ acres}}{2600 \text{ gal}}$$

Then solve for *x*:

$$x \text{ acres} = \frac{1 \text{ acre} \times 2600 \text{ gal}}{500 \text{ gal}}$$

$x = \frac{26}{5}$ **acres** or **5.2 acres**

If 35 : 5 :: 49 : x, find x.

This problem presents two equivalent ratios that can be set up in a fraction equation:

$$\frac{35}{5} = \frac{49}{x}$$

You can then cross-multiply to solve for *x*:

$$35x = 49 \times 5$$

$$x = 7$$

Percentages

A **percent** is the ratio of a part to the whole. Questions may give the part and the whole and ask for the percent, or give the percent and the whole and ask for the part, or give the part and the percent and ask for the value of the whole. The equation for percentages can be rearranged to solve for any of these:

$$percent = \frac{part}{whole}$$

$$part = whole \times percent$$

$$whole = \frac{part}{percent}$$

In the equations above, the percent should always be expressed as a decimal. In order to convert a decimal into a percentage value, simply multiply it by 100. So, if you've read 5 pages (the part) of a 10 page article (the whole), you've read $\frac{5}{10} = .50$ or 50%. (The percent sign (%) is used once the decimal has been multiplied by 100.)

Note that when solving these problems, the units for the part and the whole should be the same. If you're reading a book, saying you've read 5 pages out of 15 chapters doesn't make any sense.

Examples

45 is 15% of what number?

Set up the appropriate equation and solve. Don't forget to change 15% to a decimal value:

$$whole = \frac{part}{percent} = \frac{45}{0.15} = \mathbf{300}$$

Jim spent 30% of his paycheck at the fair. He spent $15 for a hat, $30 for a shirt, and $20 playing games. How much was his check? (Round to nearest dollar.)

Answer:

Set up the appropriate equation and solve:

$$whole = \frac{part}{percent} = \frac{15 + 30 + 20}{.30} = \mathbf{\$217.00}$$

What percent of 65 is 39?

Set up the equation and solve:

$$percent = \frac{part}{whole} = \frac{39}{65} = \mathbf{0.6 \text{ or } 60\%}$$

Greta and Max sell cable subscriptions. In a given month, Greta sells 45 subscriptions and Max sells 51. If 240 total subscriptions were sold in that month, what percent were not sold by Greta or Max?

You can use the information in the question to figure out what percentage of subscriptions were sold by Max and Greta:

$$percent = \frac{part}{whole} = \frac{51 + 45}{240} = 0.4 \text{ or } 40\%$$

However, the question asks how many subscriptions weren't sold by Max or Greta. If they sold 40%, then the other salespeople sold 100% − 40% = **60%**.

Grant needs to score 75% on an exam. If the exam has 45 questions, at least how many does he need to answer correctly to get this score?

Set up the equation and solve. Remember to convert 75% to a decimal value:

part = *whole* × *percent* = 45 × 0.75 = 33.75, so **he needs to answer at least 34 questions correctly.**

Percent Change

Percent change problems ask you to calculate how much a given quantity has changed. The problems are solved in a similar way to regular percent problems, except that instead of using the "part" you'll use the "amount of change." Note that the sign of the "amount of change" is important: if the original amount has increased the change will be positive; if it has decreased the change will be negative. Again, in the equations below the percent is a decimal value; you need to multiply by 100 to get the actual percentage.

$$percent\ change = \frac{amount\ of\ change}{original\ amount}$$

$$amount\ of\ change = original\ amount \times percent\ change$$

$$original\ amount = \frac{amount\ of\ change}{percent\ change}$$

Examples

A computer software retailer marks up its games by 40% above the wholesale price when it sells them to customers. Find the price of a game for a customer if the game costs the retailer $25.

Answer:

Set up the appropriate equation and solve:

$amount\ of\ change = original\ amount \times percent\ change\quad 10 = 25 \times 0.4$

If the amount of change is 10, that means the store adds a markup of $10, so the game costs:

$25 + $10 = **$35**

A golf shop pays its wholesaler $40 for a certain club, and then sells it to a golfer for $75. What is the markup rate?

Answer:

First, calculate the amount of change:

75 − 40 = 35

Now you can set up the equation and solve. (Note that *markup rate* is another way of saying *percent change*):

$percent\ change = \dfrac{amount\ of\ change}{original\ amount} = \dfrac{35}{40} = 0.875 = 87.5\%$

A shoe store charges a 40% markup on the shoes it sells. How much did the store pay for a pair of shoes purchased by a customer for $63?

Answer:

You're solving for the original price, but it's going to be tricky because you don't know the amount of change; you only know the new price. To solve, you need to create an expression for the amount of change:

If *original amount = x*

Then *amount of change* = 63 − *x*

Now you can plug these values into your equation:

$$original\ amount\ =\ \frac{amount\ of\ change}{percent\ change}$$

$$x\ =\ \frac{63-x}{0.4}$$

The last step is to solve for *x*:

$$0.4x\ =\ 63-x$$

$$1.4x\ =\ 63$$

$$x\ =\ 45$$

The store paid **$45** for the shoes.

An item originally priced at $55 is marked 25% off. What is the sale price?

Answer:

You've been asked to find the sale price, which means you need to solve for the amount of change first:

$$amount\ of\ change\ =\ original\ amount\ \times\ percent\ change\ =\ 55\ \times\ 0.25\ =\ 13.75$$

Using this amount, you can find the new price. Because it's on sale, we know the item will cost less than the original price:

55 − 13.75 = 41.25

The sale price is **$41.25**.

James wants to put an 18 foot by 51 foot garden in his backyard. If he does, it will reduce the size of his yard by 24%. What will be the area of the remaining yard space?

Answer:

This problem is tricky because you need to figure out what each number in the problem stands for. 24% is obviously the percent change, but what about the measurements in feet? If you multiply these values you get the area of the garden (for more on area see *Area and Perimeter*):

18 ft. × 51 ft. = 918 ft.^{2}

This 918 ft.^{2} is the amount of change—it's how much area the yard lost to create the garden. Now you can set up an equation:

$$original\ amount = \frac{amount\ of\ change}{percent\ change} = \frac{918}{24} = 3825$$

If the original lawn was 3825 ft.^{2} and the garden is 918 ft.^{2}, then the remaining area is

3825 − 918 = 2907

The remaining lawn covers **2907 ft.^{2}**

Comparison of Rational Numbers

Number comparison problems present numbers in different formats and ask which is larger or smaller, or whether the numbers are equivalent. The important step in solving these problems is to convert the numbers to the same format so that it is easier to compare them. If numbers are given in the same format, or after converting them, determine which number is smaller or if the numbers are equal. Remember that for negative numbers, higher numbers are actually smaller.

Examples

Is $4\frac{3}{4}$ greater than, equal to, or less than $\frac{18}{4}$?

Answer:

These numbers are in different formats—one is a mixed fraction and the other is just a fraction. So, the first step is to convert the mixed fraction to a fraction:

$$4\frac{3}{4} = 4 \times \frac{4}{4} + \frac{3}{4} = \frac{19}{4}$$

Once the mixed number is converted, it is easier to see that $\frac{19}{4}$ **is greater than** $\frac{18}{4}$.

Which of the following numbers has the greatest value: 104.56, 104.5, or 104.6?

Answer:

These numbers are already in the same format, so the decimal values just need to be compared. Remember that zeros can be added after the decimal without changing the value, so the three numbers can be rewritten as:

104.56

104.50

104.60

From this list, it is clearer that 104.60 is the greatest because 0.60 is larger than 0.50 and 0.56.

Is 65% greater than, less than, or equal to $\frac{13}{20}$?

Answer:

The first step is to convert the numbers into the same format. 65% is the same as $\frac{65}{100}$. Next, the fractions need to be converted to have the same denominator. It is difficult to compare fractions with different denominators. Using a factor of $\frac{5}{5}$ on the second fraction will give common denominators: $\frac{13}{20} \times \frac{5}{5} = \frac{65}{100}$. Now, is easy to see that the numbers are **equivalent**.

Exponents and Radicals

Exponents tell us how many times to multiply a base number by itself. In the example 2^4, 2 is the base number and 4 is the exponent. $2^4 = 2 \times 2 \times 2 \times 2 = 16$. Exponents are also called **powers**: 5 to the third power = $5^3 = 5 \times 5 \times 5 = 125$. Some exponents have special names: *x* to the second power is also called "*x* squared" and *x* to the third power is also called "*x* cubed." The number 3 squared = $3^2 = 3 \times 3 = 9$.

Radicals are expressions that use roots. Radicals are written in the form $\sqrt[a]{x}$, where *a* = the **radical power** and *x* = the **radicand.** The solution to the radical $\sqrt[3]{8}$ is the number that, when multiplied by itself 3 times, equals 8. $\sqrt[3]{8} = 2$ because $2 \times 2 \times 2 = 8$. When the radical power is not written we assume it is 2, so $\sqrt{9} = 3$ because $3 \times 3 = 9$. Radicals can also be written as exponents, where the power is a fraction. For example, $x^{\frac{1}{3}} = \sqrt[3]{x}$.

Review more of the rules for working with exponents and radicals in the table below.

rule	example
$x^0 = 1$	$5^0 = 1$
$x^1 = x$	$5^1 = 5$
$x^a \times x^b = x^{a+b}$	$5^2 \times 5^3 = 5^5 = 3125$
$(xy)^a = x^a y^a$	$(5 \times 6)^2 = 5^2 \times 6^2 = 900$
$(x^a)^b = x^{ab}$	$(5^2)^3 = 5^6 = 15{,}625$
$\left(\dfrac{x}{y}\right)^a = \dfrac{x^a}{y^a}$	$\left(\dfrac{5}{6}\right)^2 = \dfrac{5^2}{6^2} = \dfrac{25}{36}$
$\dfrac{x^a}{x^b} = x^{a-b} \ (x \neq 0)$	$\dfrac{5^4}{5^3} = 5^1 = 5$
$x^{-a} = \dfrac{1}{x^a} \ (x \neq 0)$	$5^{-2} = \dfrac{1}{5^2} = \dfrac{1}{25}$
$x^{1/a} = \sqrt[a]{x}$	$25^{1/2} = \sqrt[2]{25} = 5$
$\sqrt[a]{x \times y} = \sqrt[a]{x} \times \sqrt[a]{y}$	$\sqrt[3]{8 \times 27} = \sqrt[3]{8} \times \sqrt[3]{27} = 2 \times 3 = 6$
$\sqrt[a]{\dfrac{x}{y}} = \dfrac{\sqrt[a]{x}}{\sqrt[a]{y}}$	$\sqrt[3]{\dfrac{27}{8}} = \dfrac{\sqrt[3]{27}}{\sqrt[3]{8}} = \dfrac{3}{2}$
$\sqrt[a]{x^b} = x^{\frac{b}{a}}$	$\sqrt[2]{5^4} = 5^{\frac{4}{2}} = 5^2 = 25$

Examples

Simplify the expression $2^4 \times 2^2$

Answer:

When multiplying exponents in which the base number is the same, simply add the powers:

$$2^4 \times 2^2 = 2^{(4+2)} = 2^6$$

$$2^6 = 2 \times 2 \times 2 \times 2 \times 2 \times 2 = \mathbf{64}$$

Simplify the expression $(3^4)^{-1}$

Answer:

When an exponent is raised to a power, multiply the powers:

$$(3^4)^{-1} = 3^{-4}$$

When the exponent is a negative number, rewrite as the reciprocal of the positive exponent:

$$3^{-4} = \frac{1}{3^4}$$

$$\frac{1}{3^4} = \frac{1}{3 \times 3 \times 3 \times 3} = \mathbf{\frac{1}{81}}$$

Simplify the expression $\left(\frac{9}{4}\right)^{\frac{1}{2}}$

Answer:

When the power is a fraction, rewrite as a radical:

$$\left(\frac{9}{4}\right)^{\frac{1}{2}} = \sqrt{\frac{9}{4}}$$

Next, distribute the radical to the numerator and denominator:

$$\sqrt{\frac{9}{4}} = \frac{\sqrt{9}}{\sqrt{4}} = \frac{3}{2}$$

Matrices

A **matrix** is an array of numbers aligned into horizontal **rows** and vertical **columns**. A matrix is described by the number of rows (m) and columns (n) it contains. For example, a matrix with 3 rows and 4 columns is a 3 × 4 matrix.

$$\begin{bmatrix} 2 & -3 & 5 & 0 \\ 4 & -6 & 2 & 11 \\ 3.5 & 7 & 2.78 & -1.2 \end{bmatrix}$$

To add or subtract 2 matrices, simply add or subtract the corresponding numbers in each matrix. Only matrices with the same dimensions can be added or subtracted, and the resulting matrix will also have the same dimensions.

Example

Simplify: $\begin{bmatrix} 6 & 4 & -8 \\ -3 & 1 & 0 \end{bmatrix} + \begin{bmatrix} 5 & -3 & -2 \\ -3 & 4 & 9 \end{bmatrix}$

Add each corresponding number:

$$\begin{bmatrix} 6+5 & 4+(-3) & (-8)+(-2) \\ (-3)+(-3) & 1+4 & 0+9 \end{bmatrix} = \begin{bmatrix} 11 & 1 & -10 \\ -6 & 5 & 9 \end{bmatrix}$$

Solve for x and y: $\begin{bmatrix} x & 6 \\ 4 & y \end{bmatrix} + \begin{bmatrix} 3 & 2 \\ 8 & -1 \end{bmatrix} = \begin{bmatrix} 11 & 8 \\ 12 & 4 \end{bmatrix}$

Add each corresponding number to create 2 equations:

$$\begin{bmatrix} x+3 & 6+2 \\ 4+8 & y+(-1) \end{bmatrix} = \begin{bmatrix} 11 & 8 \\ 12 & 4 \end{bmatrix} \rightarrow$$

$$x + 3 = 11$$

$$y - 1 = 4$$

Now solve each equation:

$$x = 7, y = 5$$

In order to multiple 2 matrices, the number of columns in the first must equal the number of rows in the second. To multiply the matrices, multiply the numbers in each row of the first by the numbers in the column of the second and add. The resulting matrix will have the same number of rows as the first matrix and same number of columns as the second. Note that the order of the matrices is important when they're being multiplied: **AB** is not the same as **BA**.

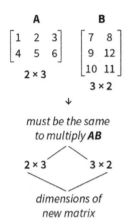

To multiply a matrix by a single number or variable, simply multiple each value within the matrix by that number or variable.

Example

If $A = \begin{bmatrix} 1 & 3 & 0 \\ 6 & 2 & 4 \end{bmatrix}$ and $B = \begin{bmatrix} 5 & 3 \\ 2 & 1 \\ 4 & 7 \end{bmatrix}$, what is **AB**?

First, check to see that they can be multiplied: A has 3 columns and B has 3 rows, so they can. The resulting matrix will be 2 × 2. Now multiply the numbers in the first row of A by the numbers in the first column of B and add the result:

$$\begin{bmatrix} 1 & 3 & 0 \\ 6 & 2 & 4 \end{bmatrix}\begin{bmatrix} 5 & 3 \\ 2 & 1 \\ 4 & 7 \end{bmatrix} = \begin{bmatrix} (1 \times 5) + (3 \times 2) + (0 \times 4) & \\ & \end{bmatrix} = \begin{bmatrix} 11 & \\ & \end{bmatrix}$$

Now multiply and add to find the 3 missing values:

$$\begin{bmatrix} 1 & 3 & 0 \\ 6 & 2 & 4 \end{bmatrix} \begin{bmatrix} 5 & 3 \\ 2 & 1 \\ 4 & 7 \end{bmatrix} = \begin{bmatrix} (1 \times 5) + (3 \times 2) + (0 \times 4) & (1 \times 3) + (3 \times 1) + (0 \times 7) \\ (6 \times 5) + (2 \times 2) + (4 \times 4) & (6 \times 3) + (2 \times 1) + (4 \times 7) \end{bmatrix} =$$

$$\begin{bmatrix} 11 & 6 \\ 50 & 48 \end{bmatrix}$$

Simplify: $6x \begin{bmatrix} 2 & -3 \\ 6 & 4 \end{bmatrix}$

Multiply each value inside the matrix by 6x:

$$6x \begin{bmatrix} 2 & -3 \\ 6 & 4 \end{bmatrix} = \begin{bmatrix} 6x \times 2 & 6x \times -3 \\ 6x \times 6 & 6x \times 4 \end{bmatrix} = \begin{bmatrix} 12x & -18x \\ 36x & 24x \end{bmatrix}$$

Algebra

The topics covered in algebra will be the most heavily tested on the **CASA**, and a basic understanding of algebra is also necessary to complete many of the questions on other topics. This chapter includes expressions, linear and quadratic equations, functions, and other topics.

Algebraic Expressions

Algebraic expressions and equations include **variables**, or letters standing in for numbers. These expressions and equations are made up of **terms**, which are groups of numbers and variables (e.g., $2xy$). An **expression** is simply a set of terms (e.g., $\frac{2x}{3yz} + 2$). When those terms are joined only by addition or subtraction, the expression is called a **polynomial** (e.g., 2x + 3yz). When working with expressions, you'll need to use many different mathematical properties and operations, including addition/subtraction, multiplication/division, exponents, roots, distribution, and the order of operations.

Evaluating Algebraic Expressions

To evaluate an algebraic expression, simply plug the given value(s) in for the appropriate variable(s) in the expression.

Example

Evaluate $2x + 6y - 3z$ *if* $x = 2, y = 4, and z = -3.$

Answer:

Plug in each number for the correct variable and simplify:

$2x + 6y - 3z = 2(2) + 6(4) - 3(-3) = 4 + 24 + 9 = 37$

Adding and Subtracting Expressions

Only **like terms**, which have the exact same variable(s), can be added or subtracted. **Constants** are numbers without variables attached, and those can be added and subtracted together as well. When simplifying an expression, like terms should be added or subtracted so that no individual group of variables occurs in more than one term. For example, the expression 5x + 6xy is in its simplest form, while 5x + 6xy – 11xy is not because the term xy appears more than once.

Examples

Simplify the expression 5xy + 7y + 2yz + 11xy – 5yz

Answer:

Start by grouping together like terms:

$(5xy + 11xy) + (2yz - 5yz) + 7y$

Now you can add together each set of like terms:

16xy + 7y – 3yz

Multiplying and Dividing Expressions

To multiply a single term by another, simply multiply the coefficients and then multiply the variables. Remember that when multiplying variables with exponents, those exponents are added together. For example, $(x^5y)(x^3y^4) = x^8y^5$.

When multiplying a term by a set of terms inside parentheses, you need to **distribute** to each term inside the parentheses as shown below:

$$\mathbf{a(b+c) = ab + ac}$$

When variables occur in both the numerator and denominator of a fraction, they cancel each other out. So, a fraction with variables in its simplest form will not have the same variable on the top and bottom.

Examples

Simplify the expression $(3x^4y^2z)(2y^4z^5)$.

> Answer:
>
> Multiply the coefficients and variables together:
>
> $3 \times 2 = 6$
>
> $y^2 \times y^4 = y^6$
>
> $z \times z^5 = z^6$
>
> Now put all the terms back together:
>
> $\mathbf{6x^4y^6z^6}$

Simplify the expression: $(2y^2)(y^3 + 2xy^2z + 4z)$

> Answer:
>
> Multiply each term inside the parentheses by the term $2y^2$:
>
> $(2y^2)(y^3 + 2xy^2z + 4z) =$
>
> $(2y^2 \times y^3) + (2y^2 \times 2xy^2z) \times (2y^2 \times 4z) =$
>
> $\mathbf{2y^5 + 4xy^4z + 8y^2z}$

Simplify the expression: (5x + 2)(3x + 3)

Answer:

Use the acronym FOIL—first, outer, inner, last—to multiply the terms:

first: $5x \times 3x = 15x^2$

outer: $5x \times 3 = 15x$

inner: $2 \times 3x = 6x$

last: $2 \times 3 = 6$

Now combine like terms:

$$15x^2 + 21x + 6$$

Simplify the expression: $\frac{2x^4y^3z}{8x^2z^2}$

Answer:

Simplify by looking at each variable and checking for those that appear in the numerator and denominator:

$$\frac{2}{8} = \frac{1}{4}$$

$$\frac{x^4}{x^2} = \frac{x^2}{1}$$

$$\frac{z}{z^2} = \frac{1}{z}$$

$$\frac{2x^4y^3z}{8x^2z^2} = \frac{x^2y^3}{4z}$$

Factoring Expressions

Factoring is splitting one expression into the multiplication of two expressions. It requires finding the **highest common factor** and dividing terms by that number. For example, in the expression $15x + 10$, the highest common factor is 5 because both terms are divisible by 5: $\frac{15x}{5} = 3x$ and $\frac{10}{5} = 2$. When you factor the expression you get $5(3x + 2)$.

Sometimes it is difficult to find the highest common factor. In these cases, consider whether the expression fits a polynomial identity. A **polynomial** is an expression with more than one term. If you can recognize the common polynomials listed below, you can easily factor the expression.

$$a^2 - b^2 = (a + b)(a - b)$$

$$a^2 + 2ab + b^2 = (a + b)(a + b) = (a + b)^2$$

$$a^2 - 2ab + b^2 = (a - b)(a - b) = (a - b)^2$$

$$a^3 + b^3 = (a + b)(a^2 - ab - b^2)$$

$$a^3 - b^3 = (a - b)(a^2 + ab + b^2)$$

Examples

Factor the expression $27x^2 - 9x$

> Answer:
>
> First, find the highest common factor. Both terms are divisible by 9:
>
> $\frac{27x^2}{9} = 3x^2$ and $\frac{9x}{9} = x$
>
> Now the expression is $9(3x^2 - x)$ – but wait, you're not done! Both terms can be divided by x:
>
> $\frac{3x^2}{x} = 3x$ and $\frac{x}{x} = 1$.
>
> The final factored expression is $\mathbf{9x(3x - 1)}$.

Factor the expression $25x^2 - 16$

> Answer:
>
> Since there is no obvious factor by which you can divide terms, you should consider whether this expression fits one of your polynomial identities.
>
> This expression is a difference of squares $a^2 - b^2$, where $a^2 = 25x^2$ and $b^2 = 16$.
>
> Recall that $a^2 - b^2 = (a + b)(a - b)$. Now solve for a and b:

$$a = \sqrt{25x^2} = 5x$$

$$b = \sqrt{16} = 4$$

$$(a + b)(a - b) = \mathbf{(5x + 4)(5x - 4)}$$

You can check your work by using the FOIL acronym to expand your answer back to the original expression:

first: $5x \times 5x = 25x^2$

outer: $5x \times -4 = -20x$

inner: $4 \times 5x = 20x$

last: $4 \times -4 = -16$

$$25x^2 - 20x + 20x - 16 = 25x^2 - 16$$

Factor the expression $100x^2 + 60x + 9$

Answer:

This is another polynomial identity, $a^2 + 2ab + b^2$. (The more you practice these problems, the faster you will recognize polynomial identities.)

$a^2 = 100x^2$, $2ab = 60x$, and $b^2 = 9$

Recall that $a^2 + 2ab + b^2 = (a + b)^2$. Now solve for a and b:

$$a = \sqrt{100x^2} = 10x$$

$$b = \sqrt{9} = 3$$

(Double check your work by confirming that $2ab = 2 \times 10x \times 3 = 60x$)

$$(a + b)^2 = \mathbf{(10x + 3)^2}$$

Linear Equations

An **equation** is a statement saying that two expressions are equal to each other. They always include an equal sign (e.g., $3x + 2xy = 17$). A **linear equation** has only two variables; on a graph, linear equations form a straight line.

Solving Linear Equations

To solve an equation, you need to manipulate the terms on each side to isolate the variable, meaning if you want to find x, you have to get the x alone on one side of the equal sign. To do this, you'll need to use many of the tools discussed above: you might need to distribute, divide, add or subtract like terms, or find common denominators.

Think of each side of the equation as the two sides of a see-saw. As long as the two people on each end weigh the same amount (no matter what it is) the see-saw will be balanced: if you have a 120 pound person on each end, the see-saw is balanced. Giving each of them a 10 pound rock to hold changes the weight on each end, but the see-saw itself stays balanced. Equations work the same way: you can add, subtract, multiply, or divide whatever you want as long as you do the same thing to both sides.

Most equations you'll see on the **CASA** can be solved using the same basic steps:

1. distribute to get rid of parentheses

2. use LCD to get rid of fractions

3. add/subtract like terms on either side

4. add/subtract so that constants appear on only one side of the equation

5. multiply/divide to isolate the variable

Examples

Solve for x: 25x + 12 = 62

Answer:

This equation has no parentheses, fractions, or like terms on the same side, so you can start by subtracting 12 from both sides of the equation:

$$25x + 12 = 62$$

$$(25x + 12) - 12 = 62 - 12$$

$$25x = 50$$

Now, divide by 25 to isolate the variable:

$$\frac{25x}{25} = \frac{50}{25}$$

$$x = 2$$

Solve the following equation for x: $2x - 4(2x + 3) = 24$

Answer:

Start by distributing to get rid of the parentheses (don't forget to distribute the negative):

$$2x - 4(2x + 3) = 24 \rightarrow$$

$$2x - 8x - 12 = 24$$

There are no fractions, so now you can join like terms:

$$2x - 8x - 12 = 24 \rightarrow$$

$$-6x - 12 = 24$$

Now add 12 to both sides and divide by −6.

$$-6x - 12 = 24 \rightarrow$$

$$(-6x - 12) + 12 = 24 + 12 \rightarrow$$

$$-6x = 36 \rightarrow$$

$$\frac{-6x}{-6} = \frac{36}{-6}$$

$$x = -6$$

Solve the following equation for x: $\frac{x}{3} + \frac{1}{2} = \frac{x}{6} - \frac{5}{12}$

Answer:

Start by multiplying by the least common denominator to get rid of the fractions:

$$\frac{x}{3} + \frac{1}{2} = \frac{x}{6} - \frac{5}{12} \rightarrow$$

$$12\left(\frac{x}{3} + \frac{1}{2}\right) = 12\left(\frac{x}{6} - \frac{5}{12}\right) \rightarrow$$

$$4x + 6 = 2x - 5$$

Now you can isolate the x:

$$(4x + 6) - 6 = (2x - 5) - 6 \rightarrow$$

$$4x = 2x - 11 \rightarrow$$

$$(4x) - 2x = (2x - 11) - 2x \rightarrow$$

$$2x = -11$$

$$x = -\frac{11}{2}$$

Find the value of x: $2(x + y) - 7x = 14x + 3$

Answer:

This equation looks more difficult because it has 2 variables, but you can use the same steps to solve for x. First, distribute to get rid of the parentheses and combine like terms:

$$2(x + y) - 7x = 14x + 3 \rightarrow$$

$$2x + 2y - 7x = 14x + 3 \rightarrow$$

$$-5x + 2y = 14x + 3$$

Now you can move the x terms to one side and everything else to the other, and then divide to isolate x:

$$-5x + 2y = 14x + 3 \rightarrow$$

$$-19x = -2y + 3 \rightarrow$$

$$x = \frac{2y - 3}{19}$$

Graphing Linear Equations

Linear equations can be plotted as straight lines on a coordinate plane. The **x-axis** is always the horizontal axis and the **y-axis** is always the vertical axis. The x-axis is positive to the right of the y-axis and negative to the left. The y-axis is positive above the x-axis and negative below. To describe the location of any point on the graph, write the coordinates in the form (x, y). The origin, the point where the x- and y-axes cross, is (0,0).

The **y-intercept** is the y coordinate where the line crosses the y-axis. The **slope** is a measure of how steep the line is. Slope is calculated by dividing the change along the y-axis by the change along the x-axis between any two points on the line.

Linear equations are easiest to graph when they are written in **point-slope form:** $y = mx + b$. The constant m represents slope and the constant b represents the y-intercept. If you know two points along the line (x_1, y_1) and (x_2, y_2), you can calculate slope using the following equation: $m = \frac{y_2 - y_1}{x_2 - x_1}$. If you know the slope and one other point along the line, you can calculate the y-intercept by plugging the number 0 in for x_2 and solving for y_2.

When graphing a linear equation, first plot the y-intercept. Next, plug in values for x to solve for y and plot additional points. Connect the points with a straight line.

Examples

Find the slope of the line: $\frac{3y}{2} + 3 = x$

> Answer:
>
> Slope is easiest to find when the equation is in point-slope form ($y = mx + b$). Rearrange the equation to isolate y:
>
> $$\frac{3y}{2} + 3 = x$$
>
> $$3y + 6 = 2x$$
>
> $$y + 2 = \frac{2x}{3}$$
>
> $$y = \frac{2x}{3} - 2$$
>
> Finally, identify the term m to find the slope of the line: $m = \frac{2}{3}$

Plot the linear equation $2y - 4x = 6$

Answer:

First, rearrange the linear equation to point-slope form ($y = mx + b$):

$2y - 4x = 6$

$y = 2x + 3$

Next, identify the y-intercept (*b*) and the slope *(m)*:

b = 3, m = 2

Now, plot the y-intercept (0, *b*) = (0, 3).

Next, plug in values for *x* and solve for *y:*

$y = 2(1) + 3 = 5 \rightarrow (1,5)$

$y = 2(-1) + 3 = 1 \rightarrow (-1,1)$

Plot these points on the graph, and connect the points with a straight line:

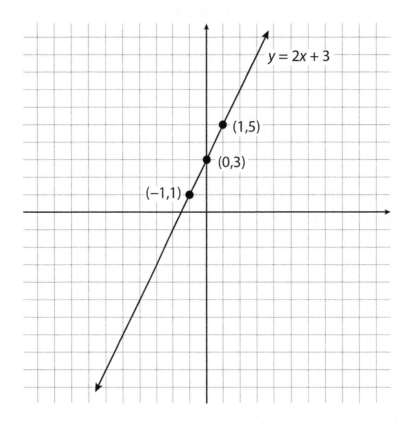

Systems of Equations

A system of equations is a group of related questions sharing the same variable. The problems you see on the **CASA** will most likely involve two equations that each have two variables, although you may also solve sets of equations with any number of variables as long as there are a corresponding number of equations (e.g., to solve a system with four variables, you need four equations).

There are two main methods used to solve systems of equations. In **substitution**, solve one equation for a single variable, then substitute the solution for that variable into the second equation to solve for the other variable. Or, you can use **elimination** by adding equations together to cancel variables and solve for one of them.

Examples

Solve the following system of equations: $3y - 4 + x = 0$ and $5x + 6y = 11$

Answer:

To solve this system using substitution, first solve one equation for a single variable:

$3y - 4 + x = 0$

$3y + x = 4$

$x = 4 - 3y$

Next, substitute the expression to the right of the equal sign for x in the second equation:

$5x + 6y = 11$

$5(4 - 3y) + 6y = 11$

$20 - 15y + 6y = 11$

$20 - 9y = 11$

$-9y = -9$

$y = 1$

Finally, plug the value for y back into the first equation to find the value of x:

$3y - 4 + x = 0$

$3(1) - 4 + x = 0$

$-1 + x = 0$

$x = 1$

The solution is $x = 1$ and $y = 1$, or the point **(1, 1)**.

Solve the system $2x + 4y = 8$ and $4x + 2y = 10$

Answer:

To solve this system using elimination, start by manipulating one equation so that a variable (in this case x) will cancel when the equations are added together:

$2x + 4y = 8$

$-2(2x + 4y = 8)$

$-4x - 8y = -16$

Now you can add the two equations together, and the x variable will drop out:

$-4x - 8y = -16$

$\underline{4x + 2y = 10}$

$-6y = -6$

$y = 1$

Lastly, plug the y value into one of the equations to find the value of x:

$2x + 4y = 8$

$2x + 4(1) = 8$

$2x + 4 = 8$

$2x = 4$

$x = 2$

The solution is $x = 2$ and $y = 1$, or the point **(2, 1)**.

Building Equations

Word problems describe a situation or a problem without explicitly providing an equation to solve. It is up to you to build an algebraic equation to solve the problem. You must translate the words into mathematical operations. Represent the quantity you do not know with a variable. If there is more than one unknown, you will likely have to write more than one equation, then solve the system of equations by substituting expressions. Make sure you keep your variables straight!

Examples

David, Jesse and Mark shoveled snow during their snow day and made a total of $100. They agreed to split it based on how much each person worked. David will take $10 more than Jesse, who will take $15 more than Mark. How much money will David get?

Answer:

Start by building an equation. David's amount will be d, Jesse's amount will be j, and Mark's amount will be m. All three must add up to $100:

$$d + j + m = 100$$

It may seem like there are three unknowns in this situation, but you can express j and m in terms of d:

Jesse gets $10 less than David, so $j = d - 10$. Mark gets $15 less than Jesse, so $m = j - 15$.

Substitute the previous expression for j to solve for m in terms of d:

$$m = (d - 10) - 15 = d - 25$$

Now back to our original equation, substituting for j and m:

$$d + (d - 10) + (d - 25) = 100$$

$$3d - 35 = 100$$

$$3d = 135$$

$$d = 45$$

David will get **$45.**

The sum of three consecutive numbers is 54. What is the middle number?

Answer:

Start by building an equation. One of the numbers in question will be *x*. The three numbers are consecutive, so if *x* is the smallest number then the other two numbers must be $(x + 1)$ and $(x - 1)$. You know that the sum of the three numbers is 54:

$$x + (x + 1) + (x + 2) = 54$$

Now solve for the equation to find *x:*

$$3x + 3 = 54$$

$$3x = 51$$

$$x = 17$$

The question asks about the middle number $(x + 1)$, so the answer is **18**.

Notice that you could have picked any number to be *x*. If you picked the middle number as *x*, your equation would be $(x - 1) + x + (x + 1) = 54$. Solve for *x* to get 18.

There are 42 people on the varsity football team. This is 8 more than half the number of people on the swim team. There are 6 fewer boys on the swim team than girls. How many girls are on the swim team?

Answer:

This word problem might seem complicated at first, but as long as you keep your variables straight and translate the words into mathematical operations you can easily build an equation. The quantity you want to solve is the number of girls on the swim team, so this will be *x*.

The number of boys on the swim team will be *y*. There are 6 fewer boys than girls so $y = x - 6$.

The total number of boys and girls on the swim team is $x + y$.

42 is 8 more than half this number, so $42 = 8 + (x + y) \div 2$

Now substitute for *y* to solve for *x*:

$$42 = 8 + (x + x - 7) \div 2$$

$$34 = (2x - 6) \div 2$$

$$68 = 2x - 6$$

$$74 = 2x$$

$$x = 37$$

There are **37** girls on the swim team.

Linear Inequalities

Inequalities look like equations, except that instead of having an equal sign, they have one of the following symbols:

> greater than: the expression left of the symbol is larger than the expression on the right

< less than: the expression left of the symbol is smaller than the expression on the right

≥ greater than or equal to: the expression left of the symbol is larger than or equal to the expression on the right

≤ less than or equal to: the expression left of the symbol is less than or equal to the expression on the right

Solving Linear Inequalities

Inequalities are solved like linear and algebraic equations. The only difference is that the symbol must be reversed when both sides of the equation are multiplied by a negative number.

Examples

Solve for x: $-7x + 2 < 6 - 5x$

Collect like terms on each side as you would for a regular equation:

$$-7x + 2 < 6 - 5x \;\rightarrow$$

$$-2x < 4$$

When you divide by a negative number, the direction of the sign switches:

$$-2x < 4 \rightarrow$$

$$x > -2$$

Graphing Linear Inequalities

Graphing a linear inequality is just like graphing a linear equation, except that you shade the area on one side of the line. To graph a linear inequality, first rearrange the inequality expression into $y = mx + b$ form. Then treat the inequality symbol like an equal sign and plot the line. If the inequality symbol is $<$ or $>$, make a broken line; for $\leq$ or $\geq$, make a solid line. Finally, shade the correct side of the graph:

For $y < mx + b$ or $y \leq mx + b$, shade the side below the line.

For $y > mx + b$ or $y \geq mx + b$, shade the side above the line.

Example

Plot the inequality $3x \geq 4 - y$

Answer:

To rearrange the inequality into $y = mx + b$ form, first subtract 4 from both sides:

$$3x - 4 \geq -y$$

Next divide both sides by –1 to get positive y; remember to switch the direction of the inequality symbol:

$$-3x + 4 \leq y$$

Now plot the line $y = -3x + 4$, making a solid line.

Finally, shade the side above the line:

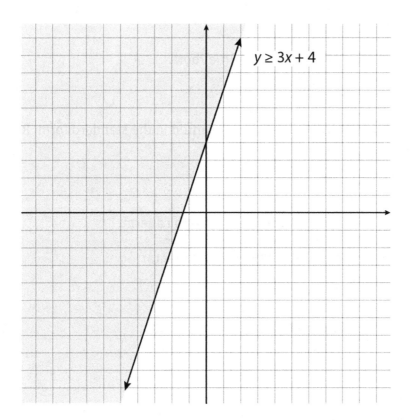

$$y \geq 3x + 4$$

Quadratic Equations

A quadratic equation is any equation in the form $ax^2 + bx + c = 0$. In quadratic equations, x is the variable and *a, b,* and *c* are all known numbers. *a* cannot be 0.

Solving Quadratic Equations

There is more than one way to solve a quadratic equation. One way is by **factoring**. By rearranging the expression $ax^2 + bx + c$ into one factor multiplied by another factor, you can easily solve for the **roots**, the values of *x* for which the quadratic expression equals 0. Another way to solve a quadratic equation is by using **the quadratic formula**: $x = \frac{-b \pm \sqrt{b^2 - 4ac}}{2a}$. The expression $b^2 - 4ac$ is called the **discriminant**; when it is positive you will get two real numbers for *x*, when it is negative you will get one real number and one imaginary number for *x*, and when it is zero you will get one real number for *x*.

Examples

Factor the quadratic equation $-2x^2 = 14x$ and find the roots.

Answer:

Not every quadratic equation you see will be presented in the standard form. Rearrange terms to set one side equal to 0:

$2x^2 + 14x = 0$

Note that a = 2, b = 14, and c = 0 because there is no third term.

Now divide the expression on the left by the common factor:

$(2x)(x + 7) = 0$

To find the roots, set each of the factors equal to 0:

$2x = 0 \rightarrow \boldsymbol{x = 0}$

$x + 7 = 0 \rightarrow \boldsymbol{x = -7}$

Use the quadratic formula to solve for x: $3x^2 = 7x - 2$

Answer:

First rearrange the equation to set one side equal to 0:

$3x^2 - 7x + 2 = 0$

Next identify the terms *a, b,* and *c*:

a = 3, b = −7, c = 2

Now plug those terms into the quadratic formula:

$$x = \frac{-b \pm \sqrt{b^2 - 4ac}}{2a}$$

$$x = \frac{7 \pm \sqrt{(-7)^2 - 4(3)(2)}}{2(3)}$$

$$x = \frac{7 \pm \sqrt{25}}{6}$$

$$x = \frac{7 \pm 5}{6}$$

Since the determinant is positive, you can expect two real numbers for x. Solve for the two possible answers:

$$x = \frac{7 + 5}{6} \rightarrow x = 2$$

$$x = \frac{7 - 5}{6} \rightarrow x = \frac{1}{3}$$

Graphing Quadratic Equations

Graphing a quadratic equation forms a **parabola**. A parabola is a symmetrical, horseshoe-shaped curve; a vertical axis passes through its vertex. Each term in the equation $ax^2 + bx + c = 0$ affects the shape of the parabola. A bigger value for a makes the curve narrower, while a smaller value makes the curve wider. A negative value for a flips the parabola upside down. The **axis of symmetry** is the vertical line $x = \frac{-b}{2a}$. To find the y-coordinate for the **vertex**, plug this value for x into the expression $ax^2 + bx + c$. The easiest way to graph a quadratic equation is to find the axis of symmetry, solve for the vertex, and then create a table of points by plugging in other numbers for x and solving for y. Plot these points and trace the parabola.

Examples

Graph the equation $x^2 + 4x + 1 = 0$

Answer:

First, find the axis of symmetry. The equation for the line of symmetry is $x = \frac{-b}{2a}$.

$$x = \frac{-4}{2(1)} = -2$$

Next, plug in −2 for x to find the y coordinate of the vertex:

$$y = (-2)^2 + 4(-2) + 1 = -3$$

The vertex is (−2, −3)

Now, make a table of points on either side of the vertex by plugging in numbers for x and solving for y:

x	$y = x^2 + 4x + 1$	(x, y)
–3	$y = (-3)^2 + 4(-3) + 1 = -2$	$(-3, -2)$
–1	$y = (-1)^2 + 4(-1) + 1 = -2$	$(-1, -2)$
–4	$y = (-4)^2 + 4(-4) + 1 = 1$	$(-4, 1)$
0	$y = (0)^2 + 4(0) + 1 = 1$	$(0, 1)$

Finally, draw the axis of symmetry, plot the vertex and your table of points, and trace the parabola:

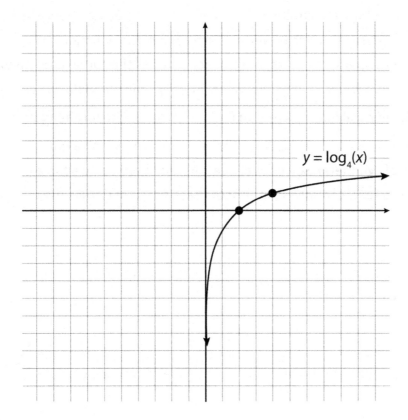

Functions

Functions describe how an input relates to an output. Linear equations, sine and cosine are examples of functions. In a function, there must be one and only one output for each input. $\sqrt{x}$ is not a function because there are two outputs for any one input: $\sqrt{4} = 2, -2$.

Describing Functions

Functions are often written in $f(x)$ form: $f(x) = x^2$ means that for input x the output is x^2. In relating functions to linear equations, you can think of $f(x)$ as equivalent to y. The **domain** of a function is all the possible inputs of that function. The **range** of a function includes the outputs of the inputs. For example, for the function $f(x) = x^2$, if the domain includes all positive and negative integers the range will include 0 and only positive integers. When you graph a function, the domain is plotted on the x-axis and the range is plotted on the y-axis.

Examples

Given $f(x) = 2x - 10$, find $f(9)$.

Answer:

Plug in 9 for x:

$f(9) = 2(9) - 10$

$f(9) = 8$

Given $f(x) = \frac{4}{x}$ with a domain of all positive integers except zero, and $g(x) = \frac{4}{x}$ with a domain of all positive and negative integers except zero, which function has a range that includes the number –2?

Answer:

The function $f(x)$ has a range of only positive numbers, since x cannot be negative. The function $g(x)$ has a range of positive and negative numbers, since x can be either positive or negative. **The number –2, therefore, must be in the range for $g(x)$ but not for $f(x)$.**

Exponential Functions

An **exponential function** is in the form $f(x) = a^x$, where $a > 0$. When $a > 1$, $f(x)$ approaches infinity as x increases and zero as x decreases. When $0 < a < 1$, $f(x)$ approaches zero as x increases and infinity as x increases. When $a = 1$, $f(x) = 1$. The graph of an exponential function where $a \neq 1$ will have a horizontal asymptote along the x-axis; the graph will never cross below the x-axis. The graph of an exponential function where $a = 1$ will be a horizontal line at $y = 1$. All graphs of exponential functions include the points $(0, 1)$ and $(1, a)$.

Examples

Graph the function $f(x) = 3^x$.

Answer:

First, estimate the shape and direction of the graph based on the value of a. Since $a > 1$, you know that $f(x)$ will approach infinity as x increases and there will be a horizontal asymptote along the negative x-axis.

Next, plot the points (0, 1) and (1, a).

Finally, plug in one or two more values for x, plot those points and trace the graph:

$f(2) = 3^2 = 9 \rightarrow (2, 9)$

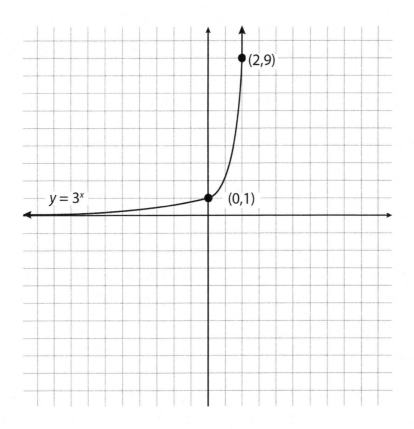

Given $f(x) = 2^x$, solve for x when $f(x) = 64$.

    Answer:

    $64 = 2^x$

    The inverse of an exponent is a log. Take the log of both sides to solve for *x*:

    $\log_2 64 = x$

    $x = 6$

Logarithmic Functions

A **logarithmic function** is the inverse of an exponential function. Remember the definition of a log: if $\log_a x = b$, then $a^b = x$. Logarithmic functions are written in the form $f(x) = \log_a x$, where *a* is any number greater than 0, except for 1. If *a* is not shown, it is assumed that *a* = 10. The function $\ln x$ is called a **natural log**, equal to $\log_e x$. When $0 < a < 1$, $f(x)$ approaches infinity as *x* approaches zero and negative infinity as *x* increases. When $a > 1$, $f(x)$ approaches negative infinity as *x* approaches zero and infinity as *x* increases. In either case, the graph of a logarithmic function has a vertical asymptote along the *y*-axis; the graph will never cross to the left of the *y*-axis. All graphs of logarithmic functions include the points (1, 0) and (*a*, 1).

Examples

Graph the function $f(x) = log_4 x$.

Answer:

First, estimate the shape and direction of the graph based on the value of *a*. Since $a > 1$, you know that $f(x)$ will approach infinity as *x* increases and there will be a vertical asymptote along the negative *y*-axis.

Next, plot the points (1, 0) and (*a*, 1).

Finally, it is easier to plug in a value for $f(x)$ and solve for *x* rather than attempting to solve for $f(x)$. Plug in one or two values for $f(x)$, plot those points and trace the graph:

$$2 = log_4 x$$

$$4^2 = x$$

$$16 = x \rightarrow (16, 2)$$

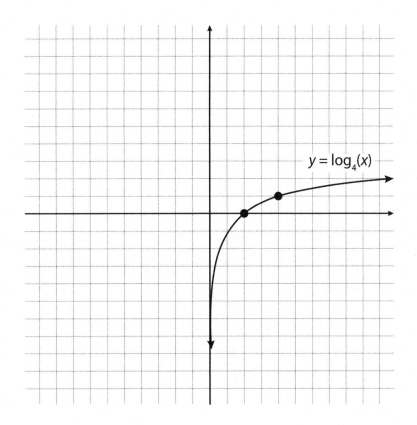

Given $f(x) = \log_{\frac{1}{3}} x$, solve for $f(81)$.

    Answer:

    Rewrite the function in exponent form:

$$x = \frac{1}{3}^{f(x)}$$

$$81 = \frac{1}{3}^{f(x)}$$

    The question is asking: to what power must you raise $\frac{1}{3}$ to get 81?

    Recognize that $3^4 = 81$, so $\frac{1}{3}^4 = \frac{1}{81}$

    Switch the sign of the exponent to flip the numerator and denominator:

$$\frac{1}{3}^{-4} = \frac{81}{1}$$

$$f(81) = -4$$

Arithmetic and Geometric Sequences

Sequences are patterns of numbers. In most questions about sequences you must determine the pattern. In an **arithmetic sequence**, add or subtract the same number between terms. In a **geometric sequence**, multiply or divide by the same number between terms. For example, 2, 6, 10, 14, 18 and 11, 4, −3, −10, −17 are arithmetic sequences because you add 4 to each term in the first example and you subtract 7 from each term in the second example. The sequence 5, 15, 45, 135 is a geometric sequence because you multiply each term by 3. In arithmetic sequences, the number by which you add or subtract is called the **common difference**. In geometric sequences, the number by which you multiply or divide is called the **common ratio**.

In an arithmetic sequence, the nth term (a_n) can be found by calculating $a_n = a_1 + (n - 1)d$, where d is the common difference and a_1 is the first term in the sequence. In a geometric sequence, $a_n = a_1(r^n)$, where r is the common ratio.

Examples

Find the common difference and the next term of the following sequence: 5, −1, −7, −13

Answer:

Find the difference between two terms that are next to each other:

$$5 - (-1) = -6$$

The common difference is −6. (It must be negative to show the difference is subtracted, not added.)

Now subtract 7 from the last term to find the next term:

$$-13 - 6 = -19$$

The next term is −19.

Find the 12th term of the following sequence: 2, 6, 18, 54

Answer:

First, decide whether this is an arithmetic or geometric sequence. Since the numbers are getting farther and farther apart, you know this must be a geometric sequence.

Divide one term by the term before it to find the common ratio:

$$18 \div 6 = 3$$

Next, plug in the common ratio and the first term to the equation $a_n = a_1(r^n)$:

$$a_{12} = 2(3^{12})$$

$$\mathbf{a_{12} = 1,062,882}$$

Notice that it would have taken a very long time to multiply each term by 3 until you got the 12th term – this is where that equation comes in handy!

The fourth term of a sequence is 9. The common difference is 11. What is the 10th term?

Answer:

To answer this question, you can simply add 9 + 11 = 20 to get the 5th term, 20 + 11 = 31 to get the 6th term, and so on until you get the 10th term. Or you can plug the information you know into your equation $a_n = a_1 + (n-1)d$. In this case, you do not know the first term. If you use the fourth term instead, you must replace $(n-1)$ with $(n-4)$:

$$a_{10} = 9 + (10 - 4)11$$

$$\mathbf{a_{10} = 75}$$

Absolute Value

The **absolute value** of a number (represented by the symbol $|x|$) is its distance from zero, not its value. For example, $|3| = 3$, and $|-3| = 3$ because both 3 and –3 are three units from zero. The absolute value of a number is always positive.

Equations with absolute values will have two answers, so you need to set up two equations. The first is simply the equation with the absolute value symbol removed. For the second equation, isolate the absolute value on one side of the equation and multiply the other side of the equation by –1.

Examples

Solve for x: |2x – 3| = x + 1

Set up the first equation by removing the absolute value symbol then solve for x:

$|2x - 3| = x + 1$

$2x - 3 = x + 1$

$x = 4$

For the second equation, remove the absolute value and multiply by –1:

$|2x - 3| = x + 1 \rightarrow$

$2x - 3 = -(x + 1) \rightarrow$

$2x - 3 = -x - 1 \rightarrow$

$3x = 2$

$x = \dfrac{2}{3}$

Both answers are correct, so the complete answer is $x = 4$ or $\dfrac{2}{3}$.

Solve for y: $2|y + 4| = 10$

Set up the first equation:

$2(y + 4) = 10$

$y + 4 = 5$

$y = 1$

Set up the second equation. Remember to isolate the absolute value before multiplying by –1:

$2|y + 4| = 10 \rightarrow$

$|y + 4| = 5 \rightarrow$

$y + 4 = -5$

$y = -9$

$$y = 1 \text{ or } -9$$

Solving Word Problems

Any of the math concepts discussed here can be turned into a word problem, and you'll likely see word problems in various forms throughout the test. (In fact, you may have noticed that several examples in the ratio and proportion sections were word problems.)

Be sure to read the entire problem before beginning to solve it: a common mistake is to provide an answer to a question that wasn't actually asked. Also, remember that not all of the information provided in a problem is necessarily needed to solve it.

When working multiple-choice word problems like those on the **CASA**, it's important to check your work. Many of the incorrect answer choices will be those resulting from common mistakes. So even if a solution you calculated is listed as an answer choice, that doesn't necessarily mean you've done the problem correctly—you have to check your own answer to be sure.

General Steps for Word Problem Solving

Step 1: Read the entire problem and determine what the question is asking.

Step 2: List all of the given data and define the variables.

Step 3: Determine the formula(s) needed or set up equations from the information in the problem.

Step 4: Solve.

Step 5: Check your answer. (Is the amount too large or small? Are the answers in the correct unit of measure?)

Key Words

Word problems generally contain key words that can help you determine what math processes may be required in order to solve them.

Addition: *added, combined, increased by, in all, total, perimeter, sum,* and *more than*

Subtraction: *how much more, less than, fewer than, exceeds, difference,* and *decreased*

Multiplication: *of, times, area,* and *product*

Division: *distribute, share, average, per, out of, percent,* and *quotient*

Equals: *is, was, are, amounts to,* and *were*

Basic Word Problems

A word problem in algebra is just an equation or a set of equations described using words. Your task when solving these problems is to turn the "story" of the problem into mathematical equations.

Examples

A store owner bought a case of 48 backpacks for $476.00. He sold 17 of the backpacks in his store for $18 each, and the rest were sold to a school for $15 each. What was the store owner's profit?

Answer:

Start by listing all the data and defining the variable:

total number of backpacks = 48

cost of backpacks = $476.00

backpacks sold in store at price of $18 = 17

backpacks sold to school at a price of $15 = 75 − 17 = 58

total profit = *x*

Now set up an equation:

$$total\ profit\ =\ income\ -\ cost$$

$$x\ =\ [(17\ \times\ 18)\ +\ (31\ \times\ 15)]\ -\ 476$$

$$x\ =\ 306\ +\ 465\ -\ 476\ =\ 295$$

The store owner made a profit of **$295**.

Thirty students in Mr. Joyce's room are working on projects over 2 days. The first day, he gave them 3/5 hour to work. On the second day, he gave them 1/2 as much time as the first day. How much time did each student have to work on the project?

Answer:

Start by listing all the data and defining your variables. Note that the number of students, while given in the problem, is not needed to find the answer:

time on 1st day = $\frac{3}{5}$ hr. = 36 min.

time on 2nd day = $\frac{1}{2}(36)$ = 18 min.

total time = x

Now set up the equation and solve:

$$total\ time\ =\ time\ on\ 1st\ day\ +\ time\ on\ 2nd\ day$$

x = 36 + 18 = 54

The students had **54 minutes** to work on the projects.

Distance Word Problems

Distance word problems involve something traveling at a constant or average speed. Whenever you read a problem that involves *how fast*, *how far*, or *for how long*, you should think of the distance equation $d = rt$, where *d* stands for distance, *r* for rate (speed), and *t* for time.

These problems can be solved by setting up a grid with *d*, *r*, and *t* along the top and each moving object on the left. When setting up the grid, make sure the units are consistent. For example, if the distance is in meters and the time is in seconds, the rate should be meters per second.

Examples

Will drove from his home to the airport at an average speed of 30 mph. He then boarded a helicopter and flew to the hospital at an average speed of 60 mph. The entire distance was 150 miles, and the trip took 3 hours. Find the distance from the airport to the hospital.

Answer:

The first step is to set up a table and fill in a value for each variable:

	d	r	t
driving	d	30	t
flying	150 – d	60	3 – t

You can now set up equations for driving and flying. The first row gives the equation $d = 30t$ and the second row gives the equation $150 - d = 60(3 - t)$.

Next, solve this system of equations. Start by substituting for d in the second equation:

$$d = 30t$$

$$150 - d = 60(30 - t) \rightarrow 150 - 30t = 60(30 - t)$$

Now solve for t:

$$150 - 30t = 180 - 60t$$

$$-30 = -30t$$

$$1 = t$$

Although you've solved for t, you're not done yet. Notice that the problem asks for distance. So, you need to solve for d: what the problem asked for. It does not ask for time, but you need to calculate it to solve the problem.

Driving: $30t = 30$ miles

Flying: $150 - d = 120$ miles

The distance from the airport to the hospital is **120 miles**.

Two riders on horseback start at the same time from opposite ends of a field that is 45 miles long. One horse is moving at 14 mph and the second horse is moving at 16 mph. How long after they begin will they meet?

Answer:

First, set up the table. The variable for time will be the same for each, because they will have been on the field for the same amount of time when they meet:

	d	r	t
Horse #1	d	14	t
Horse #2	45 − d	16	t

Next set up two equations:

Horse #1: $d = 14t$

Horse #2: $45 - d = 16t$

Now substitute and solve:

$d = 14t$

$45 - d = 16t \rightarrow 45 - 14t = 16t$

$45 = 30t$

$t = 1.5$

They will meet **1.5 hr.** after they begin.

Work Problems

Work problems involve situations where several people or machines are doing work at different rates. Your task is usually to figure out how long it will take these people or machines to complete a task while working together. The trick to doing work problems is to figure out how much of the project each person or machine completes in the same unit of time. For example, you might calculate how much of a wall a person can paint in 1 hour, or how many boxes an assembly line can pack in 1 minute.

The next step is to set up an equation to solve for the total time. This equation is usually similar to the equation for distance, but here *work = rate × time*.

Examples

Bridget can clean an entire house in 12 hours while her brother Tom takes 8 hours. How long would it take for Bridget and Tom to clean 2 houses together?

Answer:

Start by figuring out how much of a house each sibling can clean on his or her own. Bridget can clean the house in 12 hours, so she can clean $\frac{1}{12}$ of the house in an hour. Using the same logic, Tom can clean $\frac{1}{8}$ of a house in an hour.

By adding these values together, you get the fraction of the house they can clean together in an hour:

$$\frac{1}{12} + \frac{1}{8} = \frac{5}{24}$$

They can do $\frac{5}{24}$ of the job per hour.

Now set up variables and an equation to solve:

t = time spent cleaning (in hours)

h = number of houses cleaned = 2

work = rate × time

$$h = \frac{5}{24}t \;\;\rightarrow$$

$$2 = \frac{5}{24}t \;\;\rightarrow$$

$$t = \frac{48}{5} = 9\frac{3}{5}\mathbf{hr.}$$

Farmer Dan needs to water his cornfield. One hose can water a field 1.25 times faster than a second hose. When both hoses are running, they water the field together in 5 hours. How long would it take to water the field if only the slower hose is used?

Answer:

In this problem you don't know the exact time, but you can still find the hourly rate as a variable:

The second hose completes the job in f hours, so it waters $\frac{1}{f}$ field per hour. The faster hose waters the field in 1.25f, so it waters the field in $\frac{1}{1.25f}$ hours. Together, they take 5 hours to water the field, so they water $\frac{1}{5}$ of the field per hour.

Now you can set up the equations and solve:

$\frac{1}{f} + \frac{1}{1.25f} = \frac{1}{5} \rightarrow$

$1.25f \left(\frac{1}{f} + \frac{1}{1.25f}\right) = 1.25f \left(\frac{1}{5}\right) \rightarrow$

$1.25 + 1 = 0.25f$

$2.25 = 0.25f$

$f = 9$

The fast hose takes 9 hours to water the field. The slow hose takes $1.25(9) = \textbf{11.25}$ **hours**.

Martha takes 2 hours to pick 500 apples, and George takes 3 hours to pick 450 apples. How long will they take, working together, to pick 1000 apples?

Answer:

Calculate how many apples each person can pick per hour:

Martha: $\frac{500 \text{ apples}}{2 \text{ hrs}} = \frac{250 \text{ apples}}{\text{hr}}$

George: $\frac{450 \text{ apples}}{3 \text{ hrs}} = \frac{150 \text{ apples}}{\text{hr}}$

Together: $\frac{(250 + 150)\text{apples}}{\text{hr}} = \frac{400 \text{ apples}}{\text{hr}}$

Now set up an equation to find the time it takes to pick 1000 apples:

$$total\ time\ =\ \frac{1\ hr}{400\ apples}\ \times\ 1000\ apples\ =\ \frac{1000}{400}\ hrs = \textbf{2.5 hrs}$$

Geometry

Geometry is the study of shapes. On the **CASA**, you'll need to be able to find the perimeter and area of two-dimensional shapes and the volume of three-dimensional shapes. You'll also need to have a basic understanding of congruency and trigonometry.

Properties of Shapes

Area and Perimeter

Area and **perimeter** problems require you to use the equations shown in the table below to find either the area inside a shape or the distance around it (the perimeter). These equations will not be given on the test, so you need to have them memorized on test day.

Shape	Area	Perimeter
circle	$A = \pi r^2$	$C = 2\pi r = \pi d$
triangle	$A = \dfrac{b \times h}{2}$	$P = s_1 + s_2 + s_3$
square	$A = s^2$	$P = 4s$
rectangle	$A = l \times w$	$P = 2l + 2w$

Examples

A farmer has purchased 100 meters of fencing to enclose his rectangular garden. If one side of the garden is 20 meters long and the other is 28 meters long, how much fencing will the farmer have left over?

Answer:

The perimeter of a rectangle is equal to twice its length plus twice its width:

$$P = 2(20) + 2(28) = 96\ m$$

The farmer has 100 meters of fencing, so he'll have 100 – 96 = **4 meters** left.

Taylor is going to paint a square wall that is 3.5 meters high. How much paint will he need?

Each side of the square wall is 3.5 meters:

$$A = 3.5^2 = \textbf{12.25 m}$$

Volume

Volume is the amount of space taken up by a three-dimensional object. Different formulas are used to find the volumes of different shapes.

Shape	Volume
cylinder	$V = \pi r^2 h$
pyramid	$V = \dfrac{l \times w \times h}{3}$
cone	$V = \pi r^2 \dfrac{h}{3}$
sphere	$V = \dfrac{4}{3} \pi r^3$

Examples

Charlotte wants to fill her circular swimming pool with water. The pool has a diameter of 6 meters and is 1 meter deep. How many cubic meters of water will she need to fill the pool?

Answer:

This question is asking about the volume of Charlotte's pool. The circular pool is actually a cylinder, so use the formula for a cylinder: $V = \pi r^2 h$.

The diameter is 6 meters. The radius is half the diameter so $r = 6 \div 2 = 3$ meters.

Now solve for the volume:

$$V = \pi r^2 h$$

$$V = \pi (3 \text{ m})^2 (1 \text{ m})$$

$$V = 28.3 \text{ m}^3$$

Charlotte will need approximately 28.3 cubic meters of water to fill her pool.

Danny has a fishbowl that is filled to the brim with water and purchased some spherical glass marbles to line the bottom of it. He dropped in four marbles, and water spilled out of the fishbowl. If the radius of each marble is 1 centimeter, how much water spilled?

Answer:

Since the fishbowl was filled to the brim, the volume of the water that spilled out of it is equal to the volume of the marbles that Danny dropped into it. First, find the volume of one marble using the equation for a sphere:

$$V = \frac{4}{3}\pi r^3$$

$$V = \frac{4}{3}\pi (1 \text{ cm})^3$$

$$V = 4.2 \text{ cm}^3$$

Since Danny dropped in 4 marbles, multiply this volume by 4 to find the total volume:

$$4.2 \text{ cm}^3 \times 4 = 16.8 \text{ cm}^3$$

Approximately 16.8 cubic centimeters of water spilled out of the fishbowl.

Circles

The definition of a circle is the set of points that are equal distance from a center point. The distance from the center to any given point on the circle is the **radius**. If you draw a straight line segment across the circle going through the center, the distance along the line segment from one side of the circle to the other is called the **diameter**. The radius is always equal to half the diameter:

$$d = 2r$$

A **central angle** is formed by drawing radii out from the center to two points *A* and *B* along the circle. The **intercepted arc** is the portion of the circle (the arc length) between points *A* and *B*. You can find the intercepted arc length *l* if you know the central angle θ and vice versa:

$$l = 2\pi r \frac{\theta}{360°}$$

A **chord** is a line segment that connects two points on a circle. Unlike the diameter, a chord does not have to go through the center. You can find the chord length if you know either the central angle θ or the radius of the circle r and the distance from the center of the circle to the chord d (d must be at a right angle to the chord):

If you know the central angle, chord length = $2r \sin\dfrac{\theta}{2}$

If you know the radius and distance, chord length = $2\sqrt{r^2 - d^2}$

A **secant** is similar to a chord; it connects two points on a circle. The difference is that a secant is a line, not a line segment, so it extends outside of the circle on either side.

A **tangent** is a straight line that touches a circle at only one point.

A **sector** is the area within a circle that is enclosed by a central angle; if a circle is a pie, a sector is the piece of pie cut by two radii. You can find the **area of a sector** if you know either the central angle θ or the arc length l.

If you know the central angle, the area of the sector = $\pi r^2\,\dfrac{\theta}{360°}$

If you know the arc length, the area of a sector = $\dfrac{1}{2}rl$

There are two other types of angles you can create in or around a circle. **Inscribed angles** are inside the circle: the vertex is a point P on the circle and the rays extend to two other points on the circle (A and B). As long as A and B remain constant, you can move the vertex P anywhere along the circle and the inscribed angle will be the same. **Circumscribed angles** are outside of the circle: the rays are formed by two tangent lines that touch the circle at points A and B.

You can find the inscribed angle if you know the radius of the circle r and the arc length l between A and B:

inscribed angle = $\dfrac{90°l}{\pi r}$

To find the circumscribed angle, find the central angle formed by the same points A and B and subtract that angle from 180°.

Examples

A circle has a diameter of 10 centimeters. What is the intercepted arc length between points A and B if the central angle between those points measures 46°?

Answer:

First divide the diameter by two to find the radius:

$r = 10 \text{ cm} \div 2 = 5 \text{ cm}$

Now use the formula for intercepted arc length:

$$l = 2\pi r \frac{\theta}{360°}$$

$$l = 2\pi(5 \text{ cm}) \frac{46°}{360°}$$

$$l = \mathbf{4.0 \text{ cm}}$$

A chord is formed by line segment $\overline{QP}$. The radius of the circle is 5 cm and the chord length is 6 cm. Find the distance from center C to the chord.

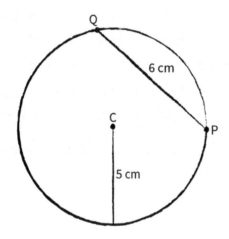

Answer:

Use the formula for chord length:

chord length = $2\sqrt{r^2 - d^2}$

In this example, we are told the chord length and the radius, and we need to solve for d:

$$6 \text{ cm} = 2\sqrt{(5 \text{ cm})^2 - d^2}$$

$$3 \text{ cm} = \sqrt{(5 \text{ cm})^2 - d^2}$$

$$9 \text{ cm}^2 = 25 \text{ cm}^2 - d^2$$

$$d^2 = 16 \text{ cm}^2$$

$$\boldsymbol{d = 4 \text{ cm}}$$

Points A and B are located on a circle. The arc length between A and B is 2 centimeters. The diameter of the circle is 8 centimeters. Find the inscribed angle.

Answer:

First, divide the diameter by two to find the radius:

$$r = \tfrac{1}{2}(8 \text{ cm})$$

$$r = 4 \text{ cm}$$

Now use the formula for an inscribed angle:

$$\text{inscribed angle} = \frac{90°l}{\pi r}$$

$$\text{inscribed angle} = \frac{90°(2 \text{ cm})}{\pi(4 \text{ cm})}$$

$$\boldsymbol{\text{inscribed angle} = 14.3°}$$

Congruence

Congruence means having the same size and shape. Two shapes are congruent if you can turn (rotate), flip (reflect), and/or slide (translate) one to fit perfectly on top of the other. Two angles are congruent if they measure the same number of degrees; they do not have to face the same direction nor must they necessarily have rays of equal length.

If two triangles have one of the combinations of congruent sides and/or angles listed below, then those triangles are congruent:

SSS – *side, side, side*

ASA – *angle, side, angle*

SAS – *side, angle, side*

AAS – *angle, angle, side*

An **isosceles triangle** has two sides of equal length. The sides of equal length are called the legs and the third side is called the base. If you bisect an isosceles triangle by drawing a line perpendicular to the base, you will form two congruent right triangles.

Where two lines cross and form an X, the opposite angles are congruent and are called **vertical angles**.

Parallel lines are lines that never cross. If you cut two parallel lines by a transversal, you will form four pairs of congruent **corresponding angles**.

A **parallelogram** is a quadrilateral in which both pairs of opposite sides are parallel and congruent (of equal length). In a parallelogram, the two pairs of opposite angles are also congruent. If you divide a parallelogram by either of the diagonals, you will form two congruent triangles.

Examples

Kate and Emily set out for a bike ride together. They ride 6 miles north, then Kate turns 90° to the west and Emily turns 90° to the east. They both ride another 8 miles. If Kate has 10 more miles to ride home, how far must Emily ride home?

Answer:

Draw out Kate's and Emily's trips to see that they form triangles. The triangles have corresponding sides with lengths of 6 miles and 8 miles, and a corresponding angle in between of 90°. This fits the "SAS" rule so the triangles must be congruent. The length Kate has to ride home corresponds to the length Emily has to ride home, so **Emily must ride 10 miles**.

Angle A measures 53°. Find angle H.

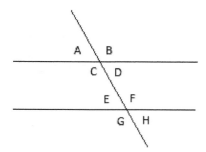

Answer:

For parallel lines cut by a transversal, look for vertical and corresponding angles.

Angles *A* and *D* are vertical angles, so angle *D* must be congruent to angle *A*. Angle *D* = 53°.

Angles *D* and *H* are corresponding angles, so angle *H* must be congruent to angle *D*. **Angle *H* = 53°.**

Right Triangles and Trigonometry

Pythagorean Theorem

Shapes with 3 sides are known as **triangles**. In addition to knowing the formulas for their area and perimeter, you should also know the Pythagorean Theorem, which describes the relationship between the three sides (*a*, *b*, and *c*) of a triangle:

$$a^2 + b^2 = c^2$$

Example

Erica is going to run a race in which she'll run 3 miles due north and 4 miles due east. She'll then run back to the starting line. How far will she run during this race?

Answer:

Start by drawing a picture of Erica's route. You'll see it forms a triangle.

One leg of the triangle is missing, but you can find its length using the Pythagorean Theorem:

$$a^2 + b^2 = c^2$$

$$3^2 + 4^2 = c^2$$

$$25 = c^2$$

$$c = 5$$

Adding all 3 sides gives the length of the whole race:

$$3 + 4 + 5 = \mathbf{12\ mi}$$

Trigonometry

Using **trigonometry**, you can calculate an angle in a right triangle based on the ratio of two sides of that triangle. You can also calculate one of the side lengths using the measure of an angle and another side. **Sine (sin), cosine (cos),** and **tangent (tan)** correspond to the three possible ratios of side lengths. They are defined below:

$$\sin \theta = \frac{opposite}{hypotenuse}$$

$$\cos \theta = \frac{adjacent}{hypotenuse}$$

$$\tan \theta = \frac{opposite}{adjacent}$$

Opposite is the side opposite from the angle θ, *adjacent* is the side adjacent to the angle θ, and *hypotenuse* is the longest side of the triangle, opposite from the right angle. SOH-CAH-TOA is an acronym to help you remember which ratio goes with which function.

When solving for a side or an angle in a right triangle, first identify which function to use based on the known lengths or angle.

Examples

Phil is hanging holiday lights. To do so safely, he must lean his 20-foot ladder against the outside of his house an angle of 15° or less. How far from the house he can safely place the base of the ladder?

Answer:

Draw a triangle with the known length and angle labeled.

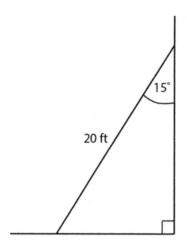

The known side (the length of the ladder) is the hypotenuse of the triangle, and the unknown distance is the side opposite the angle. Therefore, you can use sine:

$$\sin\theta = \frac{opposite}{hypotenuse}$$

$$\sin 15° = \frac{opposite}{20\text{ feet}}$$

Now solve for the opposite side:

$$opposite = \sin 15° (20\text{ feet})$$

$$\boldsymbol{opposite = 5.2\text{ feet}}$$

Grace is practicing shooting hoops. She is 5 feet 4 inches tall; her basketball hoop is 10 feet high. From 8 feet away, at what angle does she have to look up to see the hoop? Assume that her eyes are 4 inches lower than the top of her head.

Answer:

Draw a diagram and notice that the line from Grace's eyes to the hoop of the basket forms the hypotenuse of a right triangle. The side adjacent to the angle of her eyes is the distance from the basket: 8 feet. The side opposite to Grace's eyes is the difference between the height of her eyes and the height of the basket: 10 feet – 5 feet = 5 feet.

Next, use the formula for tangent to solve for the angle:

$$\tan \theta = \frac{opposite}{adjacent}$$

$$\tan \theta = \frac{5 \text{ ft}}{8 \text{ ft}}$$

Now take the inverse tangent of both sides to solve for the angle:

$$\theta = \tan^{-1} \frac{5}{8}$$

$$\boldsymbol{\theta = 32°}$$

Coordinate Geometry

Coordinate geometry is the study of points, lines, and shapes that have been graphed on a set of axes.

Points, Lines, and Planes

In coordinate geometry, points are plotted on a **coordinate plane**, a two-dimensional plane in which the **x-axis** indicates horizontal direction and the **y-axis** indicates vertical direction. The intersection of these two axes is the **origin**. Points are defined by their location in relation to the horizontal and vertical axes. The coordinates of a point are written **(x, y)**. The coordinates of the origin are (0, 0). The x coordinates to the right of the origin and the y-coordinates above it are positive; the x-coordinates to the left of the origin and the y-coordinates below it are negative.

A **line** is formed by connecting any two points on a coordinate plane; lines are continuous in both directions. Lines can be defined by their **slope**, or steepness, and their **y-intercept**, or the point at which they intersect the y-axis. A line is represented by the equation $y = mx + b$. The constant m represents slope and the constant b represents the y-intercept.

Examples

Matt parks his car near a forest where he goes hiking. From his car he hikes 1 mile north, 2 miles east, then 3 miles west. If his car represents the origin, find the coordinates of Matt's current location.

Answer:

To find the coordinates, you must find Matt's displacement along the x- and y-axes. Matt hiked 1 mile north and zero miles south, so his displacement along the y-axis is +1 mile. Matt hiked 2 miles east and 3 miles west, so his displacement along the x axis is +2 miles – 3 miles = –1 mile.

Matt's coordinates are (–1, 1).

A square is drawn on a coordinate plane. The bottom corners are located at (–2, 3) and (4, 3). What are the coordinates for the top right corner?

Answer:

Draw the coordinate plane and plot the given points. If you connect these points you will see that the bottom side is 6 units long. Since it is a square, all sides must be 6 units long. Count 6 units up from the point (4, 3) to find the top right corner.

The coordinates for the top right corner are (4, 9).

The Distance and Midpoint Formulas

To determine the distance between the points (x_1, y_1) and (x_2, y_2) from a grid use the formula $d = \sqrt{(x_2 - x_1)^2 + (y_2 - y_1)^2}$. The midpoint, which is halfway between the 2 points, is the point $\left(\frac{x_1 + x_2}{2}, \frac{y_1 + y_2}{2}\right)$.

Examples

What is the distance between points (3, –6) and (–5, 2)?

Answer:

Plug the values for x_1, x_2, y_1, and y_2 into the distance formula and simplify:

$$d = \sqrt{(-5 - 3)^2 + (2 - (-6))^2} = \sqrt{64 + 64} = \sqrt{64 \times 2} = 8\sqrt{2}$$

What is the midpoint between points (3, –6) and (–5, 2)?

Plug the values for x_1, x_2, y_1, and y_2 into the midpoint formula and simplify:

$$midpoint = \left(\frac{-5 + 3}{2}, \frac{2 + -6}{2}\right) = \left(\frac{-2}{2}, \frac{4}{2}\right) = (-1, 2)$$

Statistics and Probability

Describing Sets of Data

Statistics is the study of sets of data. The goal of statistics is to take a group of values—numerical answers from a survey, for example—and look for patterns in how that data is distributed.

When looking at a set of data, it's helpful to consider the **measures of central tendency**, a group of values that describe the central or typical data point from the set. The **CASA** covers three measures of central tendency: mean, median, and mode.

Mean is the mathematical term for *average*. To find the mean, total all the terms and divide by the number of terms. The **median** is the middle number of a given set. To find the median, put the terms in numerical order; the middle number will be the median. In the case of a set of even numbers, the middle two numbers are averaged. **Mode** is the number which occurs most frequently within a given set. If two different numbers both appear with the highest frequency, they are both the mode.

When examining a data set, also consider **measures of variability**, which describe how the data is dispersed around the central data point. The **CASA** covers two measures of variability: range and standard deviation. **Range** is simply the difference between the largest and smallest values in the set. **Standard deviation** is a measure of how dispersed the data is, or how far it reaches from the mean.

Examples

Find the mean of 24, 27, and 18.

Answer:

Add the terms, then divide by the number of terms:

$$mean = \frac{24 + 27 + 18}{3} = 23$$

The mean of three numbers is 45. If two of the numbers are 38 and 43, what is the third number?

Answer:

Set up the equation for mean with *x* representing the third number, then solve:

$$mean = \frac{38 + 43 + x}{3} = 45$$

$$\frac{38 + 43 + x}{3} = 45$$

$$38 + 43 + x = 135$$

$$x = 54$$

What is the median of 24, 27, and 18?

Answer:

Place the terms in order, then pick the middle term:

18, 24, 27

The median is **24**.

What is the median of 24, 27, 18, and 19?

Answer:

Place the terms in order. Because there is an even number of terms, the median will be the average of the middle 2 terms:

18, 19, 24, 27

$$median = \frac{19 + 24}{2} = \mathbf{21.5}$$

What is the mode of 2, 5, 4, 4, 3, 2, 8, 9, 2, 7, 2, and 2?

Answer:

The mode is **2** because it appears the most within the set.

What is the standard deviation of 62, 63, 61, and 66?

Answer:

To find the standard deviation, first find the mean:

$$mean = \frac{62 + 63 + 61 + 66}{4} = 63$$

Next, find the difference between each term and the mean, and square that number:

$$63 - 62 = 1 \rightarrow 1^2 = 1$$

$$63 - 63 = 0 \rightarrow 0^2 = 0$$

$$63 - 61 = 2 \rightarrow 2^2 = 4$$

$$63 - 66 = -3 \rightarrow (-3)^2 = 9$$

Now, find the mean of the squares: $mean = \frac{1 + 0 + 4 + 9}{4} = 3.5$

Finally, find the square root of the mean:

$$\sqrt{3.5} = 1.87$$

The standard deviation is **1.87**.

Graphs and Charts

These questions require you to interpret information from graphs and charts; they are pretty straightforward as long as you pay careful attention to detail. There are several different graph and chart types that may appear on the **CASA**.

Bar Graphs

Bar graphs present the numbers of an item that exist in different categories. The categories are shown on the *x*-axis, and the number of items is shown on the *y*-axis. Bar graphs are usually used to easily compare amounts.

Examples

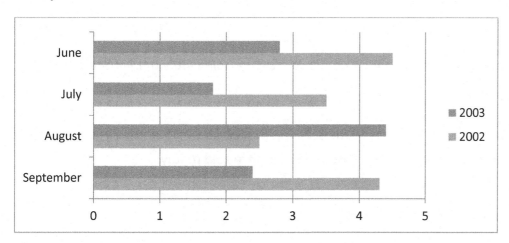

The chart above shows rainfall in inches per month. Which month had the least amount of rainfall? Which had the most?

Answer:

The shortest bar will be the month that had the least rain, and the longest bar will correspond to the month with the greatest amount: **July 2003 had the least**, and **June 2002 had the most**.

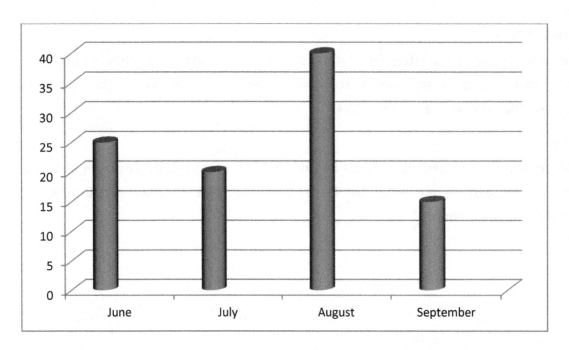

Using the chart above, how many more ice cream cones were sold in July than in September?

Answer:

Tracing from the top of each bar to the scale on the left shows that sales in July were 20 and September sales were 15. So, **5 more cones were sold in July**.

Pie Charts

Pie charts present parts of a whole, and are often used with percentages. Together, all the slices of the pie add up to the total number of items, or 100%.

Examples

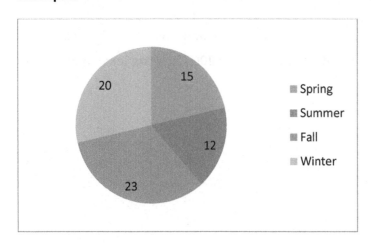

122

The pie chart above shows the distribution of birthdays in a class of students. How many students have birthdays in the spring or summer?

Answer:

15 students have birthdays in the spring and 12 in winter, so there are **27 students** with birthdays in spring or summer.

Using the same graph above, what percentage of students have birthdays in winter?

Use the equation for percent:

$$percent = \frac{part}{whole} = \frac{winter\ birthdays}{total\ birthdays} = \frac{20}{20 + 15 + 23 + 12} = \frac{20}{70} = \frac{2}{7} = .286 \text{ or } \textbf{28.6\%}$$

Line Graphs

Line graphs show trends over time. The number of each item represented by the graph will be on the *y*-axis, and time will be on the *x*-axis.

Examples

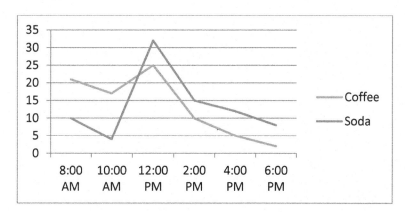

The line graph above shows beverage sales at an airport snack shop throughout the day. Which beverage sold more at 4:00 p.m.?

Answer:

At 4:00 p.m., approximately 12 sodas and 5 coffees were sold, so more **soda** was sold.

At what time of day were the most beverages sold?

> This question is asking for the time of day with the most sales of coffee and soda combined. It is not necessary to add up sales at each time of day to find the answer. Just from looking at the graph, you can see that sales for both beverages were highest at noon, so the answer must be **12:00 p.m.**

Histograms

A **histogram** shows a distribution of a variable in bar chart form. The variables on the *x*-axis is continuous and grouped into categories called bins. The frequency of results in each bin are shown on the *y*-axis. While histograms look like bar graphs, they are more similar to pie charts: they show you parts of a whole.

Examples

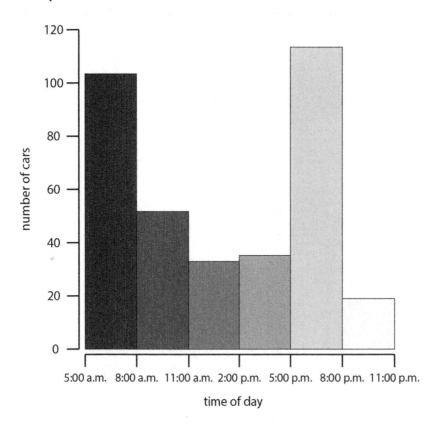

The figure above shows the number of cars that traveled through a toll plaza throughout the day. How many cars passed through the toll plaza between 8:00 a.m. and 5:00 p.m.?

To find the total number, we need to add the number of cars for each relevant time period (note that all number are approximations):

8:00 a.m. – 11:00 a.m.: 50 cars

11:00 a.m. – 2:00 p.m.: 30 cars

2:00 p.m. – 5:00 p.m.: 35 cars

50 + 30 + 35 = **115 cars**

Probability

Probability is the likelihood that an event will take place. This likelihood is expressed as a value between 0 and 1. The closer the probability is to zero, the less likely the event is to occur; the closer the probability is to 1, the more likely it is to occur.

Probability of a Single Event

The **probability** of an outcome occurring is found by dividing the number of desired outcomes by the number of total possible outcomes. As with percentages, a probability is the ratio of a part to a whole, with the whole being the total number of possibilities, and the part being the number of desired results. Probabilities can be written using percentages (40%), decimals (0.4), fractions $\left(\frac{2}{5}\right)$, or in words (the probability of an outcome is 2 in 5).

$$probability = \frac{desired\ outcomes}{total\ possible\ outcomes}$$

Examples

A bag holds 3 blue marbles, 5 green marbles, and 7 red marbles. If you pick one marble from the bag, what is the probability it will be blue?

Answer:

Because there are 15 marbles in the bag (3 + 5 + 7), the total number of possible outcomes is 15. Of those outcomes, 3 would be blue marbles, which is the desired outcome. Using that information, you can set up an equation:

$$probability = \frac{desired\ outcomes}{total\ possible\ outcomes} = \frac{3}{15} = \frac{1}{5}$$

The probability is **1 in 5** or **0.2** that a blue marble is picked.

A bag contains 75 balls. If the probability is 0.6 that a ball selected from the bag will be red, how many red balls are in the bag?

Answer:

Because you're solving for desired outcomes (the number of red balls), first you need to rearrange the equation:

$$probability = \frac{desired\ outcomes}{total\ possible\ outcomes} \rightarrow$$

$$desired\ outcomes = probability \times total\ possible\ outcomes$$

Here, choosing a red ball is the desired outcome; the total possible outcomes are represented by the 75 total balls.

$$desired\ outcomes = 0.6 \times 75 = 45$$

There are **45 red balls** in the bag.

A theater has 230 seats: 75 seats are in the orchestra area, 100 seats are in the mezzanine, and 55 seats are in the balcony. If a ticket is selected at random, what is the probability that it will be for either a mezzanine or balcony seat?

Answer:

In this problem, the desired outcome is a seat in either the mezzanine or balcony area, and the total possible outcomes are represented by the 230 total seats. So you can write this equation:

$$probability = \frac{desired\ outcomes}{total\ possible\ outcomes} = \frac{100 + 55}{230} = \mathbf{0.67}$$

The probability of selecting a student whose name begins with the letter S from a school attendance log is 7%. If there are 42 students whose names begin with S enrolled at the school, how many students in total attend it?

Because you're solving for total possible outcomes (total number of students), first you need to rearrange the equation:

$$total\ possible\ outcomes\ =\ \frac{desired\ outcomes}{probability}$$

In this problem, you are given a probability (7% or 0.07) and the number of desired outcomes (42). Plug these numbers into the equation to solve:

$$total\ possible\ outcomes\ =\ \frac{42}{0.07}\ =\ \textbf{600 students}$$

Conditional Probability

Conditional probability refers to the chances of one event occurring, given that another event has already occurred. **Independent events** are events that have no effect on one another. The classic example is flipping a coin: whether you flip heads or tails one time has no bearing on how you might flip the next time. Your chance of flipping heads is always 50/50. **Dependent events**, on the other hand, have an effect on the next event's probability. If you have a bag full of red and blue marbles, removing a red marble the first time will decrease the probability of picking a red marble the second time, since now there are fewer red marbles in the bag. The probability of event B occurring, given that event A has occurred, is written $P(B|A)$.

The probability of either event A or event B occurring is called the **union** of events A and B, written $A \cup B$. The probability of $A \cup B$ is equal to the <u>sum</u> of the probability of A occurring and the probability of B occurring, <u>minus</u> the probability of both A and B occurring. The probability of both A and B occurring is called the **intersection** of events A and B, written $A \cap B$. The probability of $A \cap B$ is equal to the <u>product</u> of the probability of A and the probability of B, given A. Review the equations for the probabilities of unions and intersections below:

$$P(A \cup B) = P(A) + P(B) - P(A \cap B)$$

$$P(A \cap B) = P(A) \times P(B|A)$$

The **complement** of an event is when the event <u>does not</u> occur. The probability of the complement of event A, written $P(A')$, is equal to $1 - P(A)$.

Examples

A bag contains 5 red marbles and 11 blue marbles. What is the probability of pulling out a blue marble, followed by a red marble?

Answer:

This question is asking about an intersection of events. The equation for an intersection of events is $P(A \cap B) = P(A) \times P(B|A)$.

The first event, event A, is picking out a blue marble. Find $P(A)$:

$$P(A) = \frac{11 \text{ blue marbles}}{16 \text{ total marbles}} = \frac{11}{16}$$

The second event, event B, is picking out a red marble, now that there are 15 marbles left. Find $P(B|A)$:

$$P(B|A) = \frac{5 \text{ red marbles}}{15 \text{ total marbles}} = \frac{5}{15} = \frac{1}{3}$$

$$P(A \cap B) = P(A) \times P(B|A) = \frac{11}{16} \times \frac{1}{3} = \mathbf{\frac{11}{48}}$$

Caroline randomly draws a playing card from a full deck. What is the chance she will select either a queen or a diamond?

Answer:

This question is asking about a union of events. The equation for a union of events is $P(A \cup B) = P(A) + P(B) - P(A \cap B)$.

The first event, event A, is selecting a queen. Find $P(A)$:

$$P(A) = \frac{4 \text{ queens}}{52 \text{ total cards}} = \frac{4}{52}$$

The second event, event B, is selecting a diamond. Find $P(B)$:

$$P(B) = \frac{13 \text{ diamonds}}{52 \text{ total cards}} = \frac{13}{52}$$

Now, find the probability of selecting a queen that is also a diamond:

$$P(A \cap B) = \frac{1 \text{ diamond queen}}{52 \text{ total cards}} = \frac{1}{52}$$

$$P(A \cup B) = P(A) + P(B) - P(A \cap B) = \frac{4}{52} + \frac{13}{52} - \frac{1}{52} = \frac{16}{52} = \frac{4}{13}$$

Chapter 3: Writing

The Writing section of the **CASA** focuses on the mechanics of writing. Here, you'll be asked to identify grammatical errors and revise sentences to make them clearer. You'll also write a short essay.

Writing (Grammar)

The multiple-choice portion of the Writing section will test your understanding of the basic rules of grammar, punctuation, spelling, and capitalization. You must be prepared to:

- match pronouns with their antecedents

- match verbs with their subjects

- ensure that verbs are in the correct tense

- spell irregular, hyphenated, and commonly misspelled words

- use correct capitalization

- distinguish between types of sentences

- correct sentence structure

- identify passive and active voice

The first step in preparing for this section of the test is to review parts of speech and the rules that accompany them. The good news is that you have been using these rules since you first began to speak; even if you don't know a lot of the technical terms, many of these rules will be familiar to you.

Parts of Speech

Nouns and Pronouns

Nouns are people, places, or things. For example, in the sentence *The hospital was very clean*, the noun is *hospital*; it is a place. **Pronouns** replace nouns and make sentences sound less repetitive. Take the sentence *Sam stayed home from school because Sam was not feeling well*. The word *Sam* appears twice in the same sentence. To avoid repetition and improve the sentence, use a pronoun instead: *Sam stayed at home because he did not feel well*.

Because pronouns take the place of nouns, they need to agree both in number and gender with the noun they replace. So, a plural noun needs a plural pronoun, and a feminine noun needs a feminine pronoun. In the first sentence of this paragraph, for example, the plural pronoun *they* replaced the plural noun *pronouns*. There will usually be several questions on the Writing section of the **CASA** that cover pronoun agreement, so it's good to get comfortable spotting pronouns.

Examples

Wrong: *If a student forgets their homework, it is considered incomplete.*

Correct: *If a student forgets his or her homework, it is considered incomplete.*

Student is a singular noun, but *their* is a plural pronoun, making the first sentence grammatically incorrect. To correct it, **replace *their* with the singular pronoun *his or her*.**

Wrong: *Everybody will receive their paychecks promptly.*

Correct: *Everybody will receive his or her paycheck promptly.*

Everybody is a singular noun, but *their* is a plural pronoun; the first sentence is grammatically incorrect. To correct it, **replace *their* with the singular pronoun *his or her*.**

Wrong: *When a nurse begins work at a hospital, you should wash your hands.*

Correct: *When a nurse begins work at a hospital, he or she should wash his or her hands.*

This sentence begins in third-person perspective and finishes in second-person perspective. To correct it, **ensure the sentence finishes with third-person perspective.**

Wrong: *After the teacher spoke to the student, she realized her mistake.*

Correct: *After Mr. White spoke to his student, she realized her mistake.* (*she* and *her* referring to student)

Correct: *After speaking to the student, the teacher realized her own mistake.* (*her* referring to teacher)

This sentence refers to a teacher and a student. But to whom does *she* refer, the teacher or the student? To improve clarity, **use specific names or state more clearly who spotted the mistake.**

Verbs

Remember the old commercial, "Verb: It's what you do"? That sums up verbs in a nutshell. A **verb** is the action of a sentence: verbs "do" things. A verb must be conjugated to match the context of the sentence; this can sometimes be tricky because English has many irregular verbs. For example, *run* is an action verb in the present tense that becomes *ran* in the past tense; the linking verb *is* (which describes a state of being) becomes *was* in the past tense.

Conjugation of the verb *to be*			
	Past	Present	Future
singular	was	is	will be
plural	were	are	will be

Verb tense must make sense in the context of the sentence. For example, the sentence *I was baking cookies and eat some dough* probably sounds strange. That's because the two verbs *was baking* and *eat* are in different tenses. *Was baking* occurred in the past; *eat*, on the other hand, occurs in the present. To correct this error, conjugate *eat* in the past tense: *I was baking cookies and ate some dough.*

Like pronouns, verbs must agree in number with the noun they refer back to. In the example above, the verb *was* refers back to the singular *I*. If the subject of the sentence was plural, it would need to be modified to read *They were baking cookies and ate some dough*. Note that the verb *ate* does not change form; this is common for verbs in the past tense.

Examples

Wrong: *The cat chase the ball while the dogs runs in the yard.*

Correct: *The cat chases the ball while the dogs run in the yard.*

Cat is singular, so it takes a singular verb (which confusingly ends with an *s*); *dogs* is plural, so **it needs a plural verb.**

Wrong: *The cars that had been recalled by the manufacturer was returned within a few months.*

Correct: *The cars that had been recalled by the manufacturer were returned within a few months.*

Sometimes the subject and verb are separated by clauses or phrases. Here, the subject *cars* is separated from the verb phrase *were returned*, making it more difficult to conjugate the verb correctly; this results in a *number error*.

Correct: *The deer hid in the trees.*

Correct: *The deer are not all the same size.*

The subject of these sentences is a *collective noun*, which describes a group of people or things. This noun can be singular if it is referring to the group as a whole or plural if it refers to each item in the group as a separate entity.

Correct: *The doctor and nurse work in the hospital.*

Correct: *Neither the nurse nor her boss was scheduled to take a vacation.*

Correct: *Either the patient or her parents complete her discharge paperwork.*

When the subject contains two or more nouns connected by *and*, that subject is plural and requires a plural verb. Singular subjects joined by *or, either/or, neither/nor, or not only/but also* remain singular; when these words join plural and singular subjects, the verb should match the closest subject.

Wrong: *Because it will rain during the party last night, we had to move the tables inside.*

Correct: *Because it rained during the party last night, we had to move the tables inside.*

All the verb tenses in a sentence need to agree both with each other and with the other information in the sentence. In the first sentence above, the tense doesn't match the other information in the sentence: *last night* indicates the past (*rained*) not the future (*will rain*).

Adjectives and Adverbs

Adjectives are words that describe a noun. Take the sentence *The boy hit the ball*. If you want to know more about the noun *ball*, then you could use an adjective to describe it: *The boy hit the red ball*. An adjective simply provides more information about a noun in a sentence.

Like adjectives, **adverbs** provide more information about a part of a sentence. Adverbs can describe verbs, adjectives, and even other adverbs. For example, in the sentence *The doctor had recently hired a new employee,* the adverb *recently* tells us more about how the action *hired* took place. Often, but not always, adverbs end in *–ly.* Remember that adverbs can never describe nouns—only adjectives can.

Adjectives, adverbs, and modifying phrases (groups of words that together modify another word) should always be placed as close as possible to the word they modify. Separating words from their modifiers can result in incorrect or confusing sentences.

Examples

Wrong: *Running through the hall, the bell rang and the student knew she was late.*

Correct: *Running through the hall, the student heard the bell ring and knew she was late.*

The phrase **running through the hall should be placed next to *student***, the noun it modifies.

Wrong: *The terrifyingly lion's loud roar scared the zoo's visitors.*

Correct: *The lion's terrifyingly loud roar scared the zoo's visitors.*

While the lion may indeed be terrifying, the word *terrifyingly* is an adverb and so can only modify a verb, an adjective or another adverb, not the noun *lion.* In the second sentence, ***terrifyingly* is modifying the adjective *loud*,** telling us more about the loudness of the lion's roar—so loud, it was terrifying.

Other Parts of Speech

Prepositions generally help describe relationships in space and time; they may express the location of a noun or pronoun in relation to other words and phrases in a sentence. For example, in the sentence *The nurse parked her car in a parking garage*, the preposition *in* describes the position of the car in relation to the garage. The noun that follows the preposition is called its *object*. In the example above, the object of the preposition *in* is the noun *parking garage*.

Conjunctions connect words, phrases, and clauses. The conjunctions summarized in the acronym FANBOYS—for, and, nor, but, or, yet, so—are called **coordinating conjunctions** and are used to join independent clauses. For example, in the sentence *The nurse prepared the patient for surgery, and the doctor performed the surgery*, the conjunction *and* joins the two independent clauses together. **Subordinating conjunctions** like *although*, *because*, and *if* join together an independent and dependent clause. In the sentence *She had to ride the subway because her car was broken*, the conjunction *because* joins together the two clauses. (Independent and dependent clauses are covered in more detail below.)

Interjections, like *wow* and *hey*, express emotion and are most commonly used in conversation and casual writing. They are often followed by *exclamation points*.

Constructing Sentences

Phrases and Clauses

A **phrase** is a group of words acting together that contain either a subject or verb, but not both. Phrases can be constructed from several different parts of speech. For example, a prepositional phrase includes a preposition and the object of that preposition (e.g., *under the table*), and a verb phrase includes the main verb and any helping verbs (e.g., *had been running*). Phrases cannot stand alone as sentences.

A **clause** is a group of words that contains both a subject and a verb. There are two types of clauses: **independent clauses** can stand alone as sentences, and **dependent clauses** cannot stand alone. Again, dependent clauses are recognizable as they begin with subordinating conjunctions.

Examples

Classify each of the following as a phrase, independent clause, or dependent clause:

1. *I have always wanted to drive a bright red sports car*

2. *under the bright sky filled with stars*

3. *because my sister is running late*

Answer:

Number 1 is an independent clause—it has a subject (*I*) and a verb (*have wanted*) and has no subordinating conjunction. **Number 2 is a phrase** made up of a preposition (*under*), its object (*sky*), and words that modify sky (*bright, filled with stars*), but lacks a conjugated verb. **Number 3 is a dependent clause**—it has a subject (*sister*), a verb (*is running*), and a subordinating conjunction (*because*).

Types of Sentences

A sentence can be classified as simple, compound, complex, or compound-complex based on the type and number of clauses it has.

Sentence Type	Number of Independent Clauses	Number of Dependent Clauses
simple	1	0
compound	2+	0
complex	1	1+
compound-complex	2+	1+

A **simple sentence** consists of only one independent clause. Because there are no dependent clauses in a simple sentence, it can be as short as two words, a subject and a verb (e.g., *I ran.*). However, a simple sentence may also contain prepositions, adjectives, and adverbs. Even though these additions can extend the length of a simple sentence, it is still considered a simple sentence as long as it doesn't contain any dependent clauses.

Compound sentences have two or more independent clauses and no dependent clauses. Usually a comma and a coordinating conjunction (*for, and, nor, but, or, yet,* and *so*) join the independent clauses, though semicolons can be used as well. For example, the sentence *My computer broke, so I took it to be repaired* is compound.

Complex sentences have one independent clause and at least one dependent clause. In the complex sentence *If you lie down with dogs, you'll wake up with fleas,* the first clause is dependent (because of the subordinating conjunction *if*), and the second is independent.

Compound-complex sentences have two or more independent clauses and at least one dependent clause. For example, the sentence *City traffic frustrates David because the streets are congested, so he is seeking an alternate route home,* is compound-complex. *City traffic frustrates David* is an independent clause, as is *he is seeking an alternate route home*; however the subordinating conjunction *because* indicates that *because the streets are so congested* is a dependent clause.

Examples

Classify: *San Francisco is one of my favorite places in the United States.*

Although the sentence is lengthy, it is **simple** because it contains only one subject and verb (*San Francisco . . . is*) modified by additional phrases.

Classify: *I love listening to the radio in the car because I enjoy loud music on the open road.*

The sentence has one independent clause (*I love . . . car*) and one dependent (*because I . . . road*), so it is **complex.**

Classify: *I wanted to get a dog, but I got a fish because my roommate is allergic to pet dander.*

This sentence has three clauses: two independent (*I wanted . . . dog* and *I got a fish*) and one dependent (*because my . . . dander*), so it is **compound-complex.**

Classify: *The game was cancelled, but we will still practice on Saturday.*

This sentence is made up of two independent clauses joined by a conjunction (*but*), so it is **compound**.

Clause Placement

In addition to the classifications above, sentences can also be defined by the location of the main clause. In a **periodic sentence**, the main idea of the sentence is held until the end. In a **cumulative sentence**, the independent clause comes first, and any modifying words or clauses follow it. (Note that this type of classification—periodic or cumulative—is not used in place of the simple, compound, complex, or compound-complex classifications. A sentence can be both cumulative and complex, for example.)

Examples

Classify: The *GED*, the *TASC*, the *SAT*, the *ACT*—*this dizzying array of exams proved no match for the determined students.*

In this sentence the main independent clause—*This...students*—is held until the very end, so it's **periodic**. Furthermore, despite its length the sentence is **simple** because it has only one subject (*dizzying array*) and verb (*proved*).

Classify: *Jessica was well-prepared for the test, for she had studied for weeks, taken practice exams, and reviewed the material with other students.*

Here, the main clause *Jessica...test* begins the sentence; the other clauses modify the main clause, providing more information about the main idea and resulting in a **cumulative** sentence. In addition, the sentence is **compound** as it links two independent clauses together with a comma and the coordinating conjunction *for*.

Punctuation

The basic rules for using the major punctuation marks are given in the table below.

Punctuation Basics		
Punctuation	Purpose	Example
period	ending sentences	Periods go at the end of complete sentences.
question mark	ending questions	What's the best way to end a sentence?
exclamation point	Indicating interjections or commands; ending sentences that show extreme emotion	Help! I'll never understand how to use punctuation!
comma	joining two independent clauses (always with a coordinating conjunction)	Commas can be used to join independent clauses, but they must always be followed by a coordinating conjunction in order to avoid a comma splice.
	setting apart introductory and nonessential words and phrases	Commas, when used properly, set apart extra information in a sentence.
	separating three or more items in a list	My favorite punctuation marks include the colon, semicolon, and period.
semicolon	joining together two independent clauses (never with a conjunction)	I love semicolons; they make sentences so concise!
colon	introducing a list, explanation, or definition	When I see a colon I know what to expect: more information.

apostrophe	form contractions	It's amazing how many people can't use apostrophes correctly.
	show possession	The students' grammar books are out of date, but the school's principal cannot order new ones yet.
quotation marks	indicate a direct quote	I said to her, "Tell me more about parentheses."

Examples

Wrong: *Her roommate asked her to pick up milk, and watermelon from the grocery store.*

Correct: *Her roommate asked her to pick up milk and watermelon from the grocery store.*

Commas are only needed when joining three items in a series; this sentence only has two (*milk* and *watermelon*).

Wrong: *The softball coach—who had been in the job for only a year, quit unexpectedly on Friday.*

Correct: *The softball coach—who had been in the job for only a year—quit unexpectedly on Friday.*

Correct: *The softball coach, who had been in the job for only a year, quit unexpectedly on Friday.*

When setting apart nonessential words and phrases, **you can use either dashes or commas, but not both**.

Wrong: *I'd like to order a hamburger, with extra cheese, but my friend says I should get a fruit salad instead.*

Correct: *I'd like to order a hamburger with extra cheese, but my friend says I should get a fruit salad instead.*

Prepositional phrases are usually essential to the meaning of the sentence, so they don't need to be set apart with commas. Here, the prepositional phrase *with extra cheese* helps the reader understand that the speaker wants a particularly unhealthy meal; however, the friend is encouraging a healthier option. Removing the prepositional phrase would limit the contrast between the burger and the salad. Note that the second comma remains because it is separating two independent clauses.

Capitalization

- The first word of a sentence is always capitalized.

- The first letter of a proper noun is always capitalized. (We're going to Chicago on Wednesday.)

- The first letter of an adjective derived from a proper noun is capitalized. (The play was described by critics as Shakespearian.)

- Titles are capitalized if they precede the name they modify. (President Obama met with Joe Biden, his vice president.)

- Months are capitalized, but not the names of the seasons. (Snow fell in March even though winter was over.)

- School subjects are not capitalized unless they are themselves proper nouns. (I will have chemistry and French tests tomorrow.)

Example

Which sentence contains an error in capitalization?

A)   She wrote many angry letters, but only senator Phillips responded to her request.

B)   Matthew lives on Main Street and takes the bus to work every weekday.

C)   Maria has always wanted to be an astronaut, so she's studying astronomy in school.

D)   Although his birthday is in February, Will decided to celebrate early by eating at Francisco's, his favorite restaurant.

Answer:

Sentence A) contains an error: the title *senator* should be capitalized when it's used in front of a name.

Point of View

A sentence's **point of view** is the perspective from which it is written. Point of view is described as either first, second, or third person.

Person	Pronouns	Who's acting?	Example
first	I, we	the writer	I take my time when shopping for shoes.
second	you	the reader	You prefer to shop online.
third	he, she, it, they	the subject	She buys shoes from her cousin's store.

First person appears when the writer's personal experiences, feelings, and opinions are an important element of the text. Second person is used when the author directly addresses the reader. Third person is most common in formal and academic writing; it creates distance between the writer and the reader. A sentence's point of view must remain consistent.

Example

Wrong: *If someone wants to be a professional athlete, you have to practice often.*

Correct: *If you want to be a professional athlete, you have to practice often.*

Correct: *If someone wants to be a professional athlete, he or she has to practice often.*

In the first sentence, the person shifts from **third (*someone*) to second (*you*).** It needs to be rewritten to be consistent.

Active and Passive Voice

Sentences can be written in active voice or passive voice. **Active voice** means that the subjects of the sentences are performing the action of the sentence. In a sentence in **passive voice**, the subjects are being acted on. The sentence *Justin wrecked my car* is in the active voice because the subject (*Justin*) is doing the action (*wrecked*). The sentence can be rewritten in passive voice by using a *to be* verb: *My car was wrecked by Justin*. Now the subject of the sentence (*car*) is being acted on. It's also possible to write the sentence so that the person performing the action is not identified: *My car was wrecked*.

Generally, good writing will avoid using passive voice. However, when it is unclear who or what performed the action of the sentence, passive voice may be the only option.

Examples

Rewrite the following sentence in active voice: *I was hit with a stick by my brother.*

First, identify the person or object performing the action (usually given in a prepositional phrase—here, *by my brother*) and make it the subject; the subject of the original sentence (*I*) becomes the object. Remove the *to be* verb: ***My brother hit me with a stick.***

Rewrite the following sentence in passive voice: *My roommate made coffee this morning.*

Here, the object (*coffee*) becomes the subject; move the original subject (*my roommate*) to a prepositional phrase at the end of the sentence. Add the *to be* verb: ***The coffee was made this morning by my roommate.***

Transitions

Transitions connect two ideas and also explain the logical relationship between them. For example, the transition *because* tells you that two things have a cause and effect relationship, while the transitional phrase *on the other hand* introduces a contradictory idea. On the **CASA** Writing section you may be asked to identify the best transition for a particular sentence, and you will definitely need to make good use of transitions in your essay.

Common Transitions						
Cause and Effect	Similarity	Contrast	Concluding	Addition	Examples	Time
as a result	also	but	briefly	additionally	in other words	after
because	likewise	however	finally	also	for example	before
consequently	similarly	in contrast	in conclusion	as well	for instance	currently
due to		on the other hand	in summary	further	to illustrate	later
if/then		nevertheless	to conclude	furthermore		recently
so		on the contrary		in addition		since
therefore		yet		moreover		subsequently
thus						then
						while

Examples

Choose the transition that would best fit in the blank.

1. Clara's car breaks down frequently. _____, she decided to buy a new one.

2. Chad scored more points than any other player on his team. _____, he is often late to practice, so his coach won't let him play in the game Saturday.

3. Miguel will often his lunch outside. _____, on Wednesday he took his sandwich to the park across from his office.

4. Alex set the table _____ the lasagna finished baking in the oven.

> *A) however*
>
> *B) for example*
>
> *C) while*
>
> *D) therefore*

Sentence 1 is describing a cause (her car breaks down) and an effect (she'll buy a new one), so the correct transition is **therefore**. Sentence 2 includes a contrast: it would make sense for Chad to play in the game, but he isn't, so the best transition is **however**. In Sentence 3, the clause after the transition is an example, so the best transition is **for example.** In Sentence 4, two things are occurring at the same time, so the best transition is **while**.

Wordiness and Redundancy

Sometimes sentences can be grammatically correct but still be confusing or poorly written. Often this problem arises when sentences are wordy or contain redundant phrasing (i.e., when several words with similar meanings are used). Often such phrases are used to make the writing seem more serious or academic when actually they can confuse the reader. On the test, you might be asked to clarify or even remove such phrases.

Some examples of excessive wordiness and redundancy include:

- I'll meet you in the *place where I parked my car.* → I'll meet you in the *parking lot.*

- *The point I am trying to make is that* the study was flawed. → The study was flawed.

- A memo was sent out *concerning the matter of* dishes left in the sink. → A memo was sent out *about* dishes left in the sink.

- The email was *brief and to the point.* → The email was *terse.*

- I don't think I'll ever *understand or comprehend* Italian operas. → I don't think I'll ever *understand* Italian operas.

Examples

Rewrite each of the following sentences to eliminate wordiness and redundancy.

1.   The game was canceled due to the fact that a bad storm was predicted.

      The game was canceled because a bad storm was predicted.

Replace the long phrase *due to the fact that* with the much shorter *because.*

2.   The possibility exists that we will have a party for my mother's birthday.

      We might have a party for my mother's birthday.

By rearranging the sentence, we can replace the phrase *the possibility exists that* with the word *might.*

3.   With the exception of our new puppy, all of our dogs have received their vaccinations.

      All of our dogs have been vaccinated except our new puppy.

The sentence can be rearranged to replace *with the exception of* with *except*. The phrase *receive their vaccinations* has also been shortened to *been vaccinated.*

4.   We threw away the broken microwave that didn't work.

We threw away the broken microwave.

If something is broken that means it doesn't work, so the phrase *that didn't work* can be removed.

5.   It was an unexpected surprise when we won the raffle.

It was a surprise when we won the raffle.

By definition, a surprise is always unexpected, so the word *unexpected* can be removed.

Homophones and Spelling

The **CASA** will include questions that ask you to identify the correct **homophone**, which is a set of words that are pronounced similarly but have different meanings. *Bawl* and *ball*, for example, are homophones. You will also be tested on spelling, so it's good to familiarize yourself with commonly misspelled words.

Writing (Essay)

On the Writing section of the **CASA** you will need to write an essay. A strong essay takes a position on an issue, addresses its complexities, presents specific ideas and examples that explain and support the position, and maintains an organized, logical structure. A good essay also includes strong vocabulary and varied sentence structure. Bear this in mind as you prepare for the **CASA**. The following sections walk through these steps and provide examples.

Writing a Thesis Statement

The thesis, or **thesis statement**, is central to the structure and meaning of an essay. It presents the writer's argument or position on an issue; in other words, it tells readers specifically what you think and what you will discuss. A strong, direct thesis statement is key to the organization of any essay.

Writing a good thesis statement is as simple as stating your idea and why you think it is true or correct.

Example

The prompt:

> *Many high schools have begun to adopt 1:1 technology programs, meaning that each school provides every student with a computing device such as a laptop or tablet. Educators who support these initiatives say that the technology allows for more dynamic collaboration and that students need to learn technology skills to compete in the job market. On the other hand, opponents cite increased distraction and the dangers of cyber-bullying or unsupervised internet use as reasons not to provide students with such devices.*

In your essay, take a position on this question. You may write about either one of the two points of view given, or you may present a different point of view on this question. Use specific reasons and examples to support your position.

Possible thesis statements:

Providing technology to every student is good for education because it allows students to learn important skills such as typing, web design, and video editing; it also gives students more opportunities to work cooperatively with their classmates and teachers.

I disagree with the idea that schools should provide technology to students because most students will simply be distracted by the free access to games and websites when they should be studying or doing homework.

In a world where technology is improving and changing at a phenomenal rate, schools have a responsibility to teach students how to navigate that technology safely and effectively; providing each student with a laptop or tablet is one way to help them do that.

Structuring the Essay

There are a few different ways to organize an essay, but some basics apply no matter what the style.

Essays may differ in how they present an idea, but they all have the same basic parts—introduction, body, and conclusion. The most common essay types are **persuasive** essays and **expository** essays. A persuasive essay takes a position on an issue and attempts to show the reader why it is correct. An expository essay explains different aspects of an issue without necessarily taking a side.

Introductions

Present your argument or idea in the introduction. Usually, the introductory paragraph ends with a **thesis statement**, which clearly sets forth the position or point the essay will prove. The introduction is a good place to bring up complexities, counterarguments and context, all of which will help the reader understand the reasoning behind your position on the issue at hand. Later, revisit those issues and wrap all of them up in the conclusion.

Example

Below is an example of an introduction. Note that it provides some context for the argument, acknowledges an opposing perspective, and gives the reader a good idea of the issue's complexities. Pay attention to the thesis statement in the last few lines, which clearly states the author's position.

> Technology has changed massively in recent years, but today's generation barely notices—high school students are already experienced with the internet, computers, apps, cameras, cell phones, and more. Teenagers must learn to use these tools safely and responsibly. Opponents of 1:1 technology programs might argue that students will be distracted or misuse the technology, but that is exactly why schools must teach them to use it. By providing technology to students, schools can help them apply it positively by creating great projects with other students, communicating with teachers and classmates, and conducting research for class projects. In a world where technology is improving and changing at a phenomenal rate, schools have a responsibility to teach students how to navigate that technology safely and effectively; providing each student with a laptop or tablet is one way to help them do that.

The Body Paragraphs

The body of an essay consists of a series of structured paragraphs. You may organize the body of your essay by creating paragraphs that describe or explain each reason you give in your thesis; addressing the issue as a problem and offering a solution in a separate paragraph; telling a story that demonstrates your point (make sure to break it into paragraphs around related ideas); or comparing and contrasting the merits of two opposing sides of the issue (make sure to draw a conclusion about which is better at the end).

Make sure that each paragraph is structurally consistent, beginning with a topic sentence to introduce the main idea, followed by supporting ideas and examples. No extra ideas unrelated to the paragraph's focus should appear. Use transition words and phrases to connect body paragraphs and improve the flow and readability of your essay.

In the following section you will find an example of a paragraph that is internally consistent and explains one of the main reasons given in one of the sample thesis statements above. Your essay should have one or more paragraphs like this to form the main body.

Conclusions

In order to end your essay smoothly, write a conclusion that reminds the reader why you were talking about these topics in the first place. Go back to the ideas in the introduction and thesis statement, but be careful not to simply restate your ideas; rather, reinforce your argument.

Example

Here is a sample conclusion paragraph that could go with the introduction above. Notice that this conclusion talks about the same topics as the introduction (changing technology and the responsibility of schools), but it does not simply rewrite the thesis.

> As technology continues to change, teens will need to adapt to it. Schools already teach young people myriad academic and life skills, so it makes sense that they would teach students how to use technology appropriately, too. Providing students with their own devices is one part of that important task, and schools should be supported in it.

Providing Supporting Evidence

Your essay requires not only structured, organized paragraphs; it must also provide specific evidence supporting your arguments. Whenever you make a general statement, follow it with specific examples that will help to convince the reader that your argument has merit. These specific examples do not bring new ideas to the paragraph; rather, they explain or defend the general ideas that have already been stated.

The following are some examples of general statements and specific statements that provide more detailed support:

General: *Students may get distracted online or access harmful websites.*

Specific: *Some students spend too much time using chat features or social media, or they get caught up in online games. Others spend time reading websites that have nothing to do with an assignment.*

Specific: *Teens often think they are hidden behind their computer screens. If teenagers give out personal information such as age or location on a website, it can lead to dangerous strangers seeking them out.*

General: *Schools can teach students how to use technology appropriately and expose them to new tools.*

Specific: *Schools can help students learn to use technology to work on class projects, communicate with classmates and teachers, and carry out research for classwork.*

Specific: *Providing students with laptops or tablets will allow them to get lots of practice using technology and programs at home, and only school districts can ensure that these tools are distributed widely, especially to students who may not have them at home.*

Example

Below is an example of a structured paragraph that uses specific supporting ideas. This paragraph supports the thesis introduced above (see *Introductions*).

> Providing students with their own laptop or tablet will allow them to explore new programs and software in class with teachers and classmates and to practice using it at home. In schools without laptops for students, classes have to visit computer labs where they share old computers often missing keys or that run so slowly they are hardly powered on before class ends. When a teacher tries to show students how to use a new tool or website, students must scramble to follow along and have no time to explore the new feature. If they can take laptops home instead, students can do things like practice editing video clips or photographs until they are perfect. They can email classmates or use shared files to collaborate even after school. If schools expect students to learn these skills, it is the schools' responsibility to provide students with enough opportunities to practice them.

This paragraph has some general statements:

... their own laptop or tablet will allow them to explore new programs and software... and to practice...

...it is the schools' responsibility to provide... enough opportunities...

It also has some specific examples to back them up:

151

...computers... run so slowly they are hardly powered on... students must scramble to follow along and have no time to explore...

They can email classmates or use shared files to collaborate...

Writing Well

Pay attention to the following details in order to ensure the clarity of your argument and to help readers understand the complexity and depth of your writing.

Transitions

Transitions are words, phrases, and ideas that help connect ideas throughout a text. You should use them between sentences and between paragraphs. Some common transitions include *then, next, in other words, as well, in addition to.* Be creative with your transitions, and make sure you understand what the transition you are using shows about the relationship between the ideas. For instance, the transition *although* implies that there is some contradiction between the first idea and the second.

Syntax

The way you write sentences is important to maintaining the reader's interest. Try to begin sentences differently. Make some sentences long and some sentences short. Write simple sentences. Write complex sentences that have complex ideas in them. Readers appreciate variety.

There are four basic types of sentences: simple, compound, complex, and compound-complex. Try to use some of each type. Be sure that your sentences make sense, though—it is better to have clear and simple writing that a reader can understand than to have complex, confusing syntax that does not clearly express the idea.

Word Choice and Tone

The words you choose influence the impression you make on readers. Use words that are specific, direct, and appropriate to the task. For instance, a formal text may benefit from complex sentences and impressive vocabulary, while it may be more appropriate to use simple vocabulary and sentences in writing intended for a young audience. Make use of strong vocabulary; avoid using vague, general words such as *good, bad, very,* or *a lot.* However, make sure that you are comfortable with the vocabulary you choose; if you are unsure about the word's meaning or its use in the context of your essay, don't use it at all.

Editing, Revising, and Proofreading

When writing a timed essay, you will not have very much time for these steps; spend any time you have left after writing the essay looking over it and checking for spelling and grammar mistakes that may interfere with a reader's understanding. Common mistakes to look out for include: subject/verb disagreement, pronoun/antecedent disagreement, comma splices and run-ons, and sentence fragments (phrases or dependent clauses unconnected to an independent clause).

Practice Test: Reading

Prompt 1:

Young Conrad's birthday was fixed for his espousals. The company was assembled in the chapel of the Castle, and everything ready for beginning the divine office, when Conrad himself was missing. Manfred, impatient of the least delay, and who had not observed his son retire, despatched one of his attendants to summon the young Prince. The servant, who had not stayed long enough to have crossed the court to Conrad's apartment, came running back breathless, in a frantic manner, his eyes staring, and foaming at the month. He said nothing, but pointed to the court.

The Castle of Otranto by Horace Walpole

1. What is the general mood of this passage?
    a. Happy
    b. Depressing
    c. Frantic
    d. Hopeful

2. On which day was Conrad to be married?
    a. The birthday of his wife.
    b. His own birthday.
    c. His father's birthday.
    d. The day after his birthday/

Prompt 2:

In the past, many cars were a manual transmission. Today, however, cars have shifted over to automatic transmission (for the most part). Shifting gears in a manual, however, is an important skill to learn if you plan to hit the road. Simply depress the clutch and then shift with the shifting lever to get the right gear. Then release the clutch and apply pressure to the gas at the same time.

3. Why have cars shifted from
    a. because manuals no longer work
    b. manuals are too complex
    c. to lower costs
    d. not enough information

4. What is the second step in shifting gears in a manual transmission?
    a. press the gas
    b. press the clutch
    c. move the shifting lever
    d. press the brake

5. What kind of transmission are most modern cars?
    a. automatic
    b. manual
    c. shifting
    d. auto gear

Prompt 3:

These visions faded when I perused, for the first time, those poets whose effusions entranced my soul and lifted it to heaven. I also became a poet and for one year lived in a paradise of my own creation; I imagined that I also might obtain a niche in the temple where the names of Homer and Shakespeare are consecrated. You are well acquainted with my failure and how heavily I bore the disappointment. But just at that time I inherited the fortune of my cousin, and my thoughts were turned into the channel of their earlier bent.

Frankenstein by Mary Shelley

6. Why did the narrator stop having "visions"?
    a. he discovered poetry
    b. he died
    c. he went to heaven
    d. his soul was lost

7. Where did the narrator live after becoming a poet?
    a. his house
    b. a paradise of his own creation
    c. a temple
    d. none of the above

Prompt 4:

Jim was going to the store to buy apples when he was sidetracked. Sally had been following him the entire time and finally decided to call out. Jim has broken up with her for a reason, and it was ridiculous to think she was still trying to get his attention.

8. Why might Jim not be happy to see Sally?
    a. he is too busy to talk to her
    b. she hates apples
    c. they broke up
    d. she hates him

Prompt 5:

The House of Representatives shall be composed of Members chosen every second Year by the People of the several States, and the Electors in each State shall have the Qualifications requisite for Electors of the most numerous Branch of the State Legislature.

The United States Constitution

9. How often are the members of the House of Representatives elected?
    a. every 4 years
    b. every 3 years
    c. every year
    d. every 2 years

Prompt 6:

When in the Course of human events, it becomes necessary for one people to dissolve the political bands which have connected them with another, and to assume among the powers of the earth, the separate and equal station to which the Laws of Nature and of Nature's God entitle them, a decent respect to the opinions of mankind requires that they should declare the causes which impel them to the separation.

The Declaration of Independence

10. What is this prompt introducing?
    a. the reasons for a separation
    b. reasons to stay together
    c. a revolution
    d. human history

11. Which of the following might mean the same as "dissolve political bands"?
    a. make a treaty
    b. get rid of the government
    c. abolish slavery
    d. move away

Prompt 7:

Vampires are known to be wary of men who have, on their person, garlic, crosses, holy water, or bibles. They tend to steer clear of these men, as they see them as dangerous to their continued existence.

12. Which of the following do vampires avoid?
    a. garlic
    b. holy water
    c. crosses
    d. all of the above

Prompt 8:

No Senator or Representative shall, during the Time for which he was elected, be appointed to any civil Office under the Authority of the United States, which shall have been created, or the Emoluments whereof shall have been encreased during such time; and no Person holding any Office under the United States, shall be a Member of either House during his Continuance in Office.

The United States Constitution

13. What is this meant to state?
    a. Representatives cannot create job for themselves and give themselves those jobs
    b. Representatives cannot be paid
    c. Representatives cannot be civil servants
    d. Representatives must quit their jobs

Prompt 9:

Today was not a good day. It all started with the rain in the morning. The windows were down on the car, so the seats got all wet. Then the call from Juliet, and the breakup. After that, I lost my job. Today was not a good day at all.

14. What was the last sign that "today was not a good day?
    a. rain
    b. car seat
    c. call from Juliet
    d. lost job

Prompt 10:

When Dr. Van Helsing and Dr. Seward had come back from seeing poor Renfield, we went gravely into what was to be done. First, Dr. Seward told us that when he and Dr. Van Helsing had gone down to the room below they had found Renfield lying on the floor, all in a heap. His face was all bruised and crushed in, and the bones of the neck were broken.

Dracula by Bram Stoker

15. What does the narrator mean by "went gravely into what was to be done"?
    a. kill each other
    b. go to a grave
    c. dig a grave
    d. make a plan

Prompt 11:

Every year the Academy Awards, or better known as The Oscars, brings together the best of the best in Hollywood. Each year since the original awards ceremony in 1929 great achievements in all areas of the film industry are recognized. Many married female actors, however, shy away from the honor of winning the *Academy Award of Merit* for either Best Actress or Best Supporting Actress. Ever since 1935, the "Oscar Curse" has proven more often than not to be alive and well.

16. What is the "Oscar Curse" that these famous ladies of Hollywood fear?
    a. They fear that after winning they will meet an untimely end.
    b. That soon after winning this prestigious award, the lady's husband will leave them.
    c. The fear is that their next movie will be a box-office disaster.
    d. They fear that once they win one, they will never again win in the same category.

Prompt 12:

According to CNN.com, Google recently announced that it is developing smart contact lenses that will measure a diabetic's glucose level by testing the person's tears. If victorious, Google will eliminate a very laborious daily routine in every diabetic's life; drawing blood from their body (usually from the side of a finger) to test their glucose levels.

17. In this paragraph, what does the word laborious mean?
    a. Consuming too much time
    b. Needing much unwelcome, often tedious, effort
    c. Needing to be done in a medical laboratory
    d. An excruciatingly painful procedure

Prompt 13:

Ikea stores have a unique section in their parking lots. They have a "family friendly" parking area. This area is located very close to the front entrance to the store. These spots have pink strollers painted on each parking spot.

18. What is implied by the term "family friendly"?
    a. It is implying that only those customers who come to shop at the store with young children or pregnant women can park in this area.
    b. That if you have an Ikea Family Membership you are welcomed to park in this area.
    c. Any family, of any age, are welcome to park in this special area.
    d. That if there are only a few spots left in this area of the parking lot, it would be nice to leave it for a vehicle with a family but not it isn't necessary; anyone can park there.

Prompt 14:

Everyone dreams of winning the lottery; one million, 25 million, even 55 million dollars. It is very easy to get caught up in the dreams associated with winning the jackpot. The realists of the world, however, are quick to remind us that we have a better chance of being hit by a car than winning big with the lottery.

19. What does the comparison of winning the lottery to being hit by a car imply?
    a. That if you don't have the good luck to win the lottery watch out because you only have bad luck and are likely to be hit by a car.
    b. It implies that it is not lucky to either win the lottery or be hit by a car.
    c. The comparison means that more people will get hit by a car than win big with the lottery.
    d. The implication is that if you are going to buy a lottery ticket, don't walk.

Prompt 15:

The United States Military Academy at West Point (USMA) is better known as The Point. Dating back to 1802, this coeducational federal service academy has trained some of the most revered and honored military leaders in American history. West Point has a Cadet Honor Code that is almost as old as the academy itself; "A Cadet will not lie, cheat, steal, or tolerate those who do."

20. What is the foundation of the Honor Code of West Point?
   a. The foundation of the Honor Code comes from a time when the United States where divided by the conflicts leading up to the American Civil War, but were training soldiers from both sides of the Mason-Dixie Line. This Code was required to prevent men from fighting amongst themselves.
   b. This code came from the *Southern Gentleman's Guide to Behavior* and introduced to men from the northern states during the early years of the academy.
   c. The Honor Code of West Point was adopted from the *British Military's Training Manual* that was created years before West Point even existed.
   d. West Point's Code of Honor dates back to the beginning of the academy when a gentle man's word was considered his bond. To break one's word was the worst possible thing a gentleman could ever do. His word was his honor, and without honor a man was nothing.

Prompt 16:

Davy Crockett is one of America's best-known folk heroes. Known for his political contributions to the State of Tennessee and the U.S. Congress, he also became famous during his own time for "larger than life" exploits that were retold through plays and in almanacs. Even following his death, Davy Crockett became growingly famous for exploits of legendary magnitude.

21. In this paragraph, what is the meaning of the word "almanacs"?
   a. An almanac is a book of information including a calendar, weather based predictions, anniversaries, and important events that is published yearly.
   b. An Almanac is another name for a book of locally developed plays that is published every couple years or so.
   c. An Almanac is a series of comics based on popular folklore that is published every five years.
   d. An almanac is a name given to stories that are handed down from one generation to another orally, not by written word.

Prompt 17:

Rosa Parks was a civil rights activist who refused to give up her seat in the colored section on a city bus for a white person when the white section of the bus was full and was subsequently arrested. *My Story*, which is her autobiography, she is quoted as saying, "People always say that I didn't give up my seat because I was [physically] tired [or] old….No, the only tired I was, was tired of giving in."

22. What implied by this quote?
   a. That she was old and tired of walking home after work each day and finally gave in and paid to take the bus home.
   b. This quote implies that Rosa Parks was not tired physically, or too old to stand on a bus, she was just tired of having to give in to the demands of white people; she was tired of segregation based on race.
   c. This quote means that people thought Rosa Parks was just too lazy to give up her seat on the bus.
   d. Rosa Parks was just stubborn that day on the bus, and her actions had nothing to do with the civil rights movement.

Prompt 18:

One island from the shores of San Francisco Bay is often referred to as "The Rock"; Alcatraz Island. The island has been home to one kind of prison or another since 1861 up until 1963. During its time as a federal prison, it is stated that no prisoner successfully escaped from Alcatraz although there were 14 attempts in that time.

23. Why were there never any successful escapes from the prison on Alcatraz Island?
   a. No one ever successfully escaped the prison because there were too many guards on duty. No man was ever left alone when outside of his cell.
   b. Alcatraz was inescapable because even if they penetrated the high-security around the prison, there was no way off the island since no boats were ever docked at the wharf.
   c. The entire premise of Alcatraz was that the men sent here were not to be rehabilitated back into society. Each and every aspect and component of the prison, the training of the guards, and the security around the rest of the island was created with the idea of keeping them on the island forever.
   d. The majority of men at the time the prison was active did not know how to swim, so those who attempted drowned in the water if they were not caught first.

Prompt 19:

When one wants to train a house-dog to ring a bell instead of barking to let its owner know it wants to go outside, there are only a few simple steps. First, when the dog is at the door, and barks take its paw and knock it against the bell that is hanging from the doorknob and only then open the door and let the dog outside. Repeat this every single time the dog barks to go outside. Eventually, depending on the stubbornness of the animal, the dog will cease barking at all and go to the bell and ring it each time it wants to go outside.

24. What is the type of training called?
    a. This type of training is called Negative Behavior Elimination Training.
    b. This training is referred to as either Classical Conditioning or Pavlovian Conditioning.
    c. This training called Positive Reinforcement Training.
    d. This type of training is called Basic Cognitive Retraining.

Prompt 20:

When we think of "rights" we think in terms of Human Rights. This refers to ideas that apply to everyone, everywhere in the world. These expectations are egalitarian and are part of a declaration called the *Universal Declaration of Human Rights* that adopted by the U.N. General Assembly in 1948 after the end of WWII.

25. In this paragraph, what does the word "egalitarian" mean?
    a. This word means that the rights contained in the *Universal Declaration of Human Rights* are to all be taken literally.
    b. Egalitarian means that ultimately these rights will also be applied to immediately to anyone and everyone who requests to be treated fairly.
    c. This word means that examples of basic human rights are included in the declaration adopted by the U.N.
    d. The word egalitarian means that Human Rights are the same for everyone, regardless of their race, nationality, or any other factors.

Prompt 21:

Each branch of the United States Armed Forces has special mottos that the soldiers live and are expected to die by. These special expressions are points of extreme pride for each member of the military.

26. What is the motto of the United States National Guard?
    a. "This We'll Defend"
    b. "Always Ready, Always There"
    c. "That Others May Live"
    d. "Not Self, but Country"

Prompt 22:

Examples of colloquialisms include Facebook, y'all, gotta, and shoulda.

27. What is the definition of a colloquialism?
    a. Words that are only used by Americans who live in the south.
    b. Words that only uneducated people say.
    c. Words that are used in an informal conversation, not a more formal discussion.
    d. Words that have recently been added to the dictionary as acceptable words to use in the American English Language.

Prompt 23:

Lieutenant Hiroo Onoda was a Japanese soldier who was sent to a small island in 1944 as an emissary. He refused to believe that Japan surrendered in WWII until his commanding officer finally traveled back to the island in 1974 and finally convinced him that the defeat was real. He then returned to Japan and received a hero's welcome.

28. In this sentence what is the definition of emissary?
    a. Emissary refers to Hiroo Onoda being an ambassador for the Japanese army.
    b. In this sentence, emissary means a secret agent or spy.
    c. The word emissary means messenger in this sentence.
    d. Emissary, in the context of this sentence, means a delegate of the Japanese government meant to establish an embassy on the island.

Prompt 24:

Milton S. Hershey was the founder of North America's largest chocolate manufacturer, now known as, The Hershey Company. It is hard to believe that, with such a large, successful business, that Hershey's first attempts in the confectionary business were such failures. After finishing a confectionary apprenticeship, he opened his own candy shop in Philadelphia; 6 years later it went out of business. He then returned home after failing to manufacture candies in New York City and in 1903 construction of a chocolate plant began in his hometown which was later renamed Hershey, Pennsylvania.

29. What is the main message of this passage?
    a. As an entrepreneur, if your first idea fails, do not give up, but move on to your next plan for success.
    b. One can only be successful in starting a flourishing business with the support of your hometown.
    c. It is more successful to manufacture chocolate than candy.
    d. If you start a worldwide profitable business in your hometown, they will rename the town in your honor.

Prompt 25:

"Beware the leader who bands the drums of war in order to whip the citizenry into a patriotic fervor, for patriotism is indeed a double-edged sword." This quote of Caesar's is completely anachronistic.

30. What does anachronistic mean in this context?
    a. This word means stolen in this sentence. This is a quote from another ruler from the time of Caesar, but not Caesar himself.
    b. Anachronistic means a quote that is pieced together from parts of speeches made by an individual. It is, therefore, a quote without any real meaning.
    c. In this sentence, the word anachronistic means that this is a true and accurate quote; not a paraphrase.
    d. The word anachronistic is defined as a quote that is not historically accurate in its context. At the time of Caesar; there were no drums of war, for example.

Prompt 26:

"A stitch in time saves nine." This is a proverbial expression that has used for hundreds of years.

31. What is this phrase referring to?
    a. This expression means that there is a "rip" of some sort in time and space and that only by repairing this rip will we save the world.
    b. When this phrase is used, the person means that by repairing a piece of clothing, you will save $9.00 on replacing the garment.
    c. This phrase refers to a broken relationship. If it is not repaired in time, it will take years (maybe even 9 years) to mend.
    d. The literal meaning of this expression means that if you stitch something up in time, you will save 9 stitches later. In other words, if you don't procrastinate, and repair something as soon as it is required, you won't have a bigger or worse job to fix at a later time.

Prompt 27:

In the Shakespearean play, **Julius Caesar**, a soothsayer calls out to Caesar with the following quote; *"Beware the Ides of March!"*

32. What did this declaration of the soothsayer mean?
    a. The soothsayer was warning the ruler of his impending betrayal and death at the hands of some of his most trusted men.
    b. This phrase was actually warning the crowd, not Caesar that on ever Ides of March the ruler must choose one human sacrifice to offer up to the Roman gods to guarantee prosperity for the coming year.
    c. The Ides of March was a day of celebration in the Roman Empire to commemorate the deaths of the Christians in the Coliseum. The soothsayer was merely thanking Caesar for the day of celebration. The word "Beware" has been shown to be translated incorrectly into English.
    d. The soothsayer meant to warn Caesar not to upset or anger the god for whom the month of March was named; Mars, the god of war. To upset the god Mars, was to ensure plague, famine, or other ruin.

Prompt 28:

Tornados occur when air begins to rotate and comes into contact with both the earth and a cloud at the same time. Although the size and shape of tornados vary widely, one can usually see a funnel stretching from the sky down to land. Most tornados are accompanied with winds as fast as 110 miles per hour and extreme ones can have winds as fast as 300 miles per hour. The path of a tornado is hard to predict, but it is becoming possible to detect them just before or as they form with the continued collection of data through radar and "storm chasers".

33. Storm chasing is a dangerous profession so why do people continue to put their lives in danger this way?
    a. Storm Chasers are an interesting breed of people who seek the thrill and adventure that comes along with this profession, much like extreme sports.
    b. News channels will pay large sums of money for good video of tornados, so, although it is a dangerous profession, the money is worth the risk.
    c. It is very important to discover as much as possible about how tornados work so that ultimately, scientists will detect them earlier and give people more advanced warning to get to safety. More advanced warning is the only way more lives will be saved.
    d. For statistics reasons, it is important to get first-hand data during a tornado. This way they can be compared to other natural disasters such as hurricanes and tsunamis.

Prompt 29:

"Secret Santa Sings Special Song for Sweetheart" is an example of alliteration.

34. What does "alliteration" mean?
    a. Alliteration means that the sentence has more than one meaning.
    b. Alliteration means that people with a stutter would have difficulty saying this sentence.
    c. Alliteration means that most of the words in the sentence begin with the same letter.
    d. In this sentence "alliteration" means that a secret Santa *literally* sang a special song for his sweetheart; it means that this even actually happened.

Prompt 30:

The Schneider Family was not your average family. Three generations lived in one house; Mom and Dad, four of their children, and Mom's parents who were well into their "golden years."

35. The term "golden years" is a nice way of meaning what?
    a. The term "golden years" refers to the best years of someone's life.
    b. This phrase means that the mom's parents were old or elderly people.
    c. "Golden years" is another way of saying, when they were rich.
    d. In this paragraph, the meaning of the term "golden years" means that the grandparents were spending their years taking care of everyone else in the family.

Prompt 31:

Jim had been on the road for 36 hours straight to meet an important client and hopefully finalize a huge new account for his advertising agency. After checking into his hotel, he intended just to drop off his suitcases and go down to the restaurant for a late supper. Once he entered the room, however, the cozy couch looked so friendly and welcoming to the weary traveler. Personification is a literary device that gives human characteristics to a non-human object.

36. What phrase in this paragraph is an example of personification?
    a. An example from this paragraph that is personification is, "the cozy couch looked so friendly and welcoming...."
    b. "Jim had been on the road for 36 hours straight...." is an example of personification in this paragraph.
    c. The phrase, "...and hopefully, finalize a huge new account for his advertising agency." is an example of personification.
    d. An example of personification, in this paragraph, is, "...to just drop off his suitcase and go down to the restaurant...."

37. Of the phrases below, which one is an example of an oxymoron?
    a. Three of the employees were "let go" due to suspicion of stealing money from the cash drawer.
    b. The stormy night was perfect for this woman's current mood.
    c. It was raining "cats and dogs" when the school bell rang.
    d. The community center was collecting "useless treasures" for their upcoming garage sale.

Prompt 32:

Between April 1860 and October 1861 **The Pony Express** delivered mail, news, and other forms of communication from Missouri across the Great Plains, through the Rocky Mountains, through the desert lands of Nevada to California, using only man and horse power. The Pony Express closed in October of 1861; just two days after the transcontinental telegraph reached Salt Lake City, therefore, connecting Omaha, and Nebraska to California. Other telegraph lines connect many other cities along the Pony Express Route.

38. Why did the Pony Express close?
    a. The Civil War stopped them from running their business.
    b. Another company was faster and took over the business.
    c. The Pony Express riders were unable to pass through the Rocky Mountains in the winter months.
    d. With the transcontinental telegraph connecting so many cities along the route, the Pony Express became redundant.

Prompt 33:

Between 1914 and 1935, George Herman "Babe" Ruth Jr. was known as "the Bambino" to baseball fans. Over his 22 seasons, he only played for three teams (Boston Red Sox, New York Yankees, and Boston Braves) and was known most for his hitting skills and RBI's statistics. Due mostly to Babe Ruth's hitting ability baseball changed during the 1920's from a fast-playing game with lower scores to one of higher scores and a slower pace.

39. How did "The Bambino's" hitting skills and RBI's statistics affect the way baseball was played?
    a. He hit so many batters in that the game went faster.
    b. The innings lasted longer with so many batters scoring runs.
    c. They had to stop the game because every time Babe Ruth hit a home run fans mobbed him.
    d. 'The Regulations changed which caused the game to last longer.

Prompt 34:

Kraft Macaroni and Cheese goes by many names. In Canada, it is called Kraft Dinner and in the United Kingdom it is known as Cheesy Pasta. No matter what name it is called by, this pasta dish has been a staple of the typical North American diet since its beginning in 1937. James Lewis Kraft, a Canadian living in Chicago struck gold by introducing this product during WWII, when more and more women were working outside of the home, milk and other dairy foods were rationed and hearty "meatless" meals were relied upon.

40. Why has this product continued to be a staple in our diet over 75 years after it was introduced to Americans?
    a. Most Americans love pasta and cheese.
    b. It is still the cheapest pasta on the market.
    c. The same factors that made its introduction so popular still exist today.
    d. It is still popular today because of brilliant marketing strategies.

Practice Test: Mathematics

1. A woman's dinner bill comes to $48.30. If she adds a 20% tip, what will she pay in total?
   a. $9.66
   b. $38.64
   c. $68.30
   d. $57.96

2. Simplify the expression $\frac{x^5}{(x^2)^{-1}}$.
   a) x^3

   b) $x^{3/2}$

   c) $\frac{1}{x^{3/2}}$

   d) x^7

3. Adam is painting the outside of a 4-walled shed. The shed is 5 feet wide, 4 feet deep, and 7 feet high. How much paint will Adam need?
   a. $126\ ft^2$
   b. $140\ ft^3$
   c. $63\ ft^2$
   d. 46 feet

4. A courtyard garden has flower beds in the shape of 4 equilateral triangles arranged so that their bases enclose a square space in the middle for a fountain. If the space for the fountain has an area of 1 square meter, find the total area of the flower beds and fountain space.
   A) $1.73\ m^2$
   B) $2.73\ m^2$
   C) $1.43\ m^2$
   D) $3\ m^2$

5. $2.31 * 10^2 =$

    a. 23.1

    b. 231

    c. 2310

    d. 23100

6. If $f(x) = |x - 28|$, evaluate $f(-12)$.

    a. -16

    b. 40

    c. 16

    d. -40

7. Simplify the expression $5(x^2)^{10}$.

    a. $5x^{20}$

    b. $5x^{12}$

    c. $5x^{-8}$

    d. $50x^2$

8. What is 15% of 986?

    a. 146.9

    b. 98.6

    c. 9.86

    d. 147.9

9. A circular swimming pool has a circumference of 49 feet. What is the diameter of the pool?

    a. 15.6 feet

    b. 12.3 feet

    c. 7.8 feet

    d. 17.8 feet

10. 50% of 94 is:

    a. 42

    b. 52

    c. 45

    d. 47

11. If $\angle A$ measures $57°$, find $\angle G$.

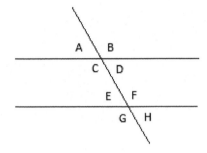

    a. $57°$

    b. $147°$

    c. $123°$

    d. $33°$

12. The table below shows the number of hours worked by employees during the week. What is the median number of hours worked per week by the employees?

Employee	Suzanne	Joe	Mark	Ellen	Jill	Rob	Nicole	Deb
Hours worked per week	42	38	25	50	45	46	17	41

    a. 38

    b. 41

    c. 42

    d. 41.5

13. Multiply the following terms: $(11xy)(2x^2y)$
   a. $13xy + x$
   b. $22x^3y^2$
   c. $44x^3y^3$
   d. $22xy^2 + 2x^2$

14. y = 2x – 5. x = 10. What is y?
   a.   10
   b.   20
   c.   15
   d.   5

15. x=2, y = -3, z = 4. Solve x+y*z
   a.   -4
   b.   10
   c.   -12
   d.   -10

16. Factor the expression $64 - 100x^2$.
   a. $(8 + 10x)(8 - 10x)$
   b. $(8 + 10x)^2$
   c. $(8 - 10x)^2$
   d. $(8 + 10x)(8x + 10)$

17. Which expression would you solve first in the following: (9+9) x 987 + 4^6
   a. 4^6
   b.   (9+9)
   c.   9 X 987
   d.   987 + 4

18. Solve for y: $10y - 8 - 2y = 4y - 22 + 5y$
   a. $y = -4\frac{2}{3}$
   b. $y = 14$
   c. $y = 30$
   d. $y = -30$

19. Solve for x: $(2x + 6)(3x - 15) = 0$

    a. $x = -5,3$

    b. $x = -3,5$

    c. $x = -2,-3$

    d. $x = -6,15$

20. Round 0.1938562 to the nearest tenth.

    a. 0.0

    b. 0.2

    c. 0.19

    d. 0.194

21. Points B and C are on a circle, and a chord is formed by line segment $\overline{BC}$. If the distance from the center of the circle to point B is 10 centimeters, and the distance from the center of the circle to the center of line segment $\overline{BC}$ is 8 centimeters, what is the length of line segment $\overline{BC}$?

    a. 6 centimeters

    b. 4 centimeters

    c. 12 centimeters

    d. 14 centimeters

22. If $f(x) = 3^x - 2$, evaluate $f(5)$.

    a. 27

    b. 243

    c. 241

    d. 13

23. If a spherical water balloon is filled with 113 milliliters of water, what is the approximate radius of the balloon? (Note: The volume, V, of a sphere with radius r is found using the equation $V = \frac{4}{3}\pi r^3$.)

    a. 4.0 centimeters

    b. 3.0 centimeters

    c. 3.6 centimeters

    d. 3.3 centimeters

24. Simplify 13/26 into a decimal.

   a. 0.13
   b. 0.16
   c. 0.5
   d. 0.25

25. Factor the expression 100x^2+25x.

   a. 100x(x+25x)
   b. 25(4x+x)
   c. 25x(4x+1)
   d. 25(4x^2+x)

26. F(x)=6x-3, G(x)=3x+4
    What will be F(3)-G(2) equal to?

   a. 4
   b. 3
   c. 5
   d. 2

27. If data set A has a standard deviation larger than the standard deviation of data set B, which of the following is true?

   a.   Data set A has more data points than data set B.
   b.   Data set A has a mean larger than the mean of data set B.
   c.   Data set A has data points clustered closer to the mean than data set B.
   d.   Data set A has data points scattered farther from the mean than data set B.

28. Solve for x: $72x^2 > 36x$

   a) $x > 0.5, x < 0$
   b) $0 < x < 0.5$
   c) $x < 0$
   d) $0 < x < 2$

29. The remainder is 3 when we divide one number by another number. What can be these two numbers from the following?

   a. 9, 5
   b. 8, 5
   c. 9, 6
   d. both B & C

30. If A and B are odd integers. Which of the following expressions must give an odd integer?
   a. A×B
   b. A+B
   c. A-B
   d. Both options A & C

31. $\frac{4}{5} \div \ldots \ldots = 2$

Which of the following will fill the blank?
   a. $\frac{2}{5}$
   b. $\frac{5}{2}$
   c. $\frac{1}{5}$
   d. Both A & C

32. Given is a set {2, 4, 6, 8........50}

   How many numbers in the given set are completely divisible by 3?
   a. 6
   b. 8
   c. 7
   d. 9

33. Find the area of a rectangular athletic field that is 100 meters long and 45 meters wide.

   A)   290 meters

   B)   4,500 m^2

   C)   145 m^2

   D)   4.5 km^2

34. Solve for x: $16x^2 + 8x + 1 = 0$

 A) $x = -\frac{1}{4}$

 B) $x = -\frac{1}{4}, \frac{1}{4}$

 C) $x = -4,4$

 D) $x = 1,4$

35. A point is located in coordinate system at (1, 2). What will be the location of this point if it is shifted 5 units downwards and 3 units in the right direction?
   a. (6, -1)
   b. (-4, 5)
   c. Remains same
   d. (4, -3)

36. $\dfrac{y+2}{3y^2+2y} + \dfrac{2y-1}{6y^3+4y^2} = \ldots\ldots\ldots$

   a. $\dfrac{2y^2+6y-1}{6y^3+4y^2}$

   b. $\dfrac{2y^2+8y-1}{6y^3+4y^2}$

   c. $\dfrac{2y^2+6y-1}{3y^2+2y}$

   d. $\dfrac{2y^2+8y-1}{3y^2+2y}$

37. If each side of the square has been increased by 1 cm and the area has now become 36cm^2. What will be the length of one side of the square before?
   a. 4 cm
   b. 5 cm
   c. 6 cm
   d. 7 cm

38. $(9)^{-3} = \ldots\ldots$
   a. $\dfrac{1}{9}$

   b. $-\dfrac{1}{(9)^3}$

   c. $\dfrac{1}{(9)^{-3}}$

   d. $\dfrac{1}{(9)^3}$

39. What is the degree of polynomial $5x^2y-5x^2y^2+5x^3y^2$?
   a. 12
   b. 4
   c. 8
   d. 5

40. Which one of the following numbers is not divisible by 3?
   a. 2352
   b. 3243
   c. 6143
   d. 5232

Practice Test: Writing

Passage 1:

Examining the impact my lifestyle has on the earth's resources is, I believe, a fascinating and valuable thing to do (1). According to the Earth Day Network ecological footprint calculator, it would take four planet earths to sustain the human population if everyone used as many resources as I do (2). My "ecological footprint," or the amount of productive area of the earth that is required to produce the resources I consume, is therefore larger than the footprints of most of the population (3). It is hard to balance the luxuries and opportunities I have available to me with doing what I know to be better from an ecological standpoint (4).

It is fairly easy for me to recycle, so I do it, but it would be much harder to forgo the opportunity to travel by plane or eat my favorite fruits that have been flown to the supermarket from a different country (5). Although I get ecological points for my recycling habits, my use of public transportation, and living in an apartment complex rather than a free-standing residence, <u>my footprint expands when it is taken into account my not-entirely-local diet</u>, my occasional use of a car, my three magazine subscriptions, and my history of flying more than ten hours a year (6). I feel that realizing just how unfair my share of the earth's resources have been should help me to change at least some of my bad habits (7).

1. Which of the following is the most concise and clear version of sentence 1?
    a. It is fascinating and valuable to examine the impact my lifestyle has on the earth's resources.
    b. Examining the impact my lifestyle has on the earth's resources is a fascinating and valuable thing to do.
    c. To examine the impact my lifestyle has on the earth's resources is fascinating and is also valuable.
    d. The impact of my lifestyle on the earth's resources is fascinating and valuable to examine.

2. How could sentences 2 and 3 best be combined?

    a. According to the Earth Day Network ecological footprint calculator, it would take four planet earths to sustain the human population if everyone used as many resources as I do because I have a very large "ecological footprint," which is the amount of productive area of the earth that is required to produce the resources I consume.

    b. According to the Earth Day Network ecological footprint calculator, which calculates the amount of productive area of the earth that is required to produce the resources one consumes, it would take four planet earths to sustain the human population if everyone had a footprint as large as mine.

    c. According to the Earth Day Network ecological footprint calculator, it would take four planet earths to sustain the human population if everyone used as many resources as I do; my "ecological footprint," or the amount of productive area of the earth that is required to produce the resources I consume, is therefore larger than the footprints of most of the population.

    d. According to the Earth Day Network ecological footprint calculator, which measures the amount of productive area of the earth that is required to produce the resources a person consumes, my footprint is larger than that of most: it would take four planet earths to sustain the human population if everyone consumed as much as I do.

3. Sentence 4 would best fit if it were moved where in this composition?

    a. at the beginning of paragraph 2

    b. after sentence 5

    c. after sentence 6

    d. at the end of paragraph 2

4. Which two sentences would be improved by switching positions?

    a. 1 and 2

    b. 3 and 4

    c. 5 and 6

    d. 6 and 7

5. Which of the following should replace the underlined portion of sentence 6?

    a. my footprint expands when one takes into account my not-entirely-local diet

    b. my footprint expands when taken into account are my not-entirely-local diet

    c. my footprint expands when we take into account my not-entirely-local diet

    d. my footprint expands when it takes into account my not-entirely-local diet

6. Which revision would most improve sentence 7?

    a. eliminate the phrase "I feel that"

    b. change "should help me" to "will help me"

    c. add the phrase "In conclusion," to the beginning

    d. change "have been" to "has been"

Passage 2:

The following questions are based on the short passage below, which is excerpted from Thomas Huxley's preface to his *Collected Essays: Volume V* (public domain) and modified slightly. Sentences are numbered at the end for easy reference within the questions.

I had set out on a journey, with no other purpose than that of exploring a certain province of natural knowledge, I strayed no hair's breadth from the course which it was my right and my duty to pursue; and yet I found that, whatever route I took, before long, I came to a tall and formidable-looking fence (1). Confident I might be in the existence of an ancient and indefeasible right of way, before me stood the thorny barrier with its comminatory notice-board—"No Thoroughfare. By order" (2). There seemed no way over; nor did the prospect of creeping round, as I saw some do, attracts me (3). True there was no longer any cause to fear the spring guns and man-traps set by former lords of the manor; but one is apt to get very dirty going on all-fours (4). The only alternatives were either to give up my journey—which I was not minded to do—or to break the fence down and go through it (5). I swiftly ruled out crawling under as an option (6). I also ruled out turning back (7).

7. How could sentence 1 best be changed?
   a. the comma after journey should be removed
   b. the comma after knowledge should be changed to a semicolon
   c. "and yet" should be eliminated
   d. change "I had set out" to "I set out"

8. Sentence 6 should be placed where in the passage?
   a. after sentence 1
   b. after sentence 2
   c. after sentence 3
   d. after sentence 4

9. Which edit should be made in sentence 3?
   a. "nor" should be changed to "or"
   b. "seemed" should be changed to "seems"
   c. "me" should be changed to "I"
   d. "attracts" should be changed to "attract"

10. How could sentences 6 and 7 best be combined?
    a. Swiftly, I ruled out crawling under as an option and also turning back.
    b. Ruling out two options swiftly: crawling under and turning back.
    c. I swiftly ruled out the options of crawling under or turning back.
    d. I ruled out crawling under as an option and I swiftly also ruled out turning back.

11. Which word could be inserted at the beginning of sentence 2 before "confident" to best clarify the meaning?
    a. Even
    b. However
    c. Hardly
    d. Finally

12. Which of the following is the best way to split sentence 1 into two separate sentences?

    a. I had set out on a journey, with no other purpose than that of exploring a certain province of natural knowledge. I strayed no hair's breadth from the course which it was my right and my duty to pursue; and yet I found that, whatever route I took, before long, I came to a tall and formidable-looking fence.

    b. I had set out on a journey, with no other purpose than that of exploring a certain province of natural knowledge, I strayed no hair's breadth from the course which it was my right and my duty to pursue. Yet I found that, whatever route I took, before long, I came to a tall and formidable-looking fence.

    c. I had set out on a journey, with no other purpose than that of exploring a certain province of natural knowledge, I strayed no hair's breadth from the course which it was my right and my duty to pursue; and yet I found that, whatever route I took, before long. I came to a tall and formidable-looking fence.

    d. I had set out on a journey. With no other purpose than that of exploring a certain province of natural knowledge, I strayed no hair's breadth from the course which it was my right and my duty to pursue; and yet I found that, whatever route I took, before long, I came to a tall and formidable-looking fence.

    e. I had set out on a journey, with no other purpose than that of exploring a certain province of natural knowledge, I strayed no hair's breadth from the course which it was my right and my duty to pursue; and yet. I found that, whatever route I took, before long, I came to a tall and formidable-looking fence.

Passage 3:

Who doesn't love a good cat meme? (1) It turns out that cats are more popular around the world than anyone had realized; with the proliferation of YouTube and social media, cats have taken the internet by storm. (2) From Grumpy Cat to Waffles, from the United States to Japan, cats appear in funny pictures, hilarious videos, and have even gone on to make their owners millions of dollars. (3)

Until recently, it had been believed that dogs were the most popular pet in the United States, with cats lagging behind in second place. (4) Dogs, "man's best friend," can be trained to do certain tricks and tasks, can be fun workout companions who play Frisbee and fetch with their owners, and can even help protect property. (5) While cats may have their uses in pest control, they are often reluctant to work on command, and very few are willing to submit to the humiliation of a collar and leash for a walk outside. (6) Still, it turns out that their funny antics and remarkable athletic prowess, even indoors, make for good TV.

(7) And so the internet is filled with cats large and small, lean and fat, wearing pieces of bread, making playthings out of boxes, jumping to amazing heights, and just looking hilariously grumpy. (8) Cats of internet fame now appear at conventions and festivals around the world, and people wait in line for hours just for a glimpse at their favorite feline celebrity. (9)

13. Which sentence <u>best</u> completes the first paragraph in order to create a good transition between two paragraphs?
    a. But cats have not always been in the spotlight; in fact, they had been relegated to a secondary position in the known hierarchy of pet popularity in popular culture.
    b. Indeed, cats are taking the world by storm.
    c. Cats are by far the most popular pet in the world, and cat ownership continues to rise.
    d. Thanks to the internet, cat marketability is becoming a field requiring true expertise, and there are even entrepreneurs who specialize in representing felines and their owners in public relations.

14. Which revision <u>more concisely</u> revises sentences (6) and (7)?
    a. No change
    b. On the other hand, cats are useful for pest control, they are often reluctant to work on command, and very few are willing to submit to the humiliation of a collar and leash for a walk outside. (6) However, it turns out that their funny antics and remarkable athletic prowess, even indoors, make for good TV. (7)
    c. Cats are useful for pest control, but they are often reluctant to work on command; moreover, very few are willing to submit to the humiliation of a collar and leash for a walk outside. (6) But it turns out that cats are more interesting—and funnier—than anyone realized, and their antics make for good TV. (7)
    d. Cats are funnier and more interesting than dogs, but are only good for pest control—they won't go for walks on leashes or learn commands.

15. What would be the <u>best</u> sentence to follow sentence 9, in keeping with the theme of the entire paragraph?

    a. Some dog owners are getting in on the act too, filming their dogs doing funny things and putting them on YouTube, but they don't get nearly as many hits as the cats do...at least not yet.

    b. Some of the cat owners have become quite media-savvy, and their cats now grace everything from coffee mugs to key chains to t-shirts; while waiting in line, fans are often enticed to buy these trinkets, but this irritates some fans.

    c. Some commentators believe that the cat owners are exploiting their cats, who no doubt would prefer to be at home napping in the sun or chasing mice.

    d. We mourn internet sensations like Chairman Meow who have passed on, and laud newcomers like Smushyface who have risen to the challenge of feline fame.

16. What would be a good title for this essay, keeping in mind both the topic and the tone?

    a. The Rise and Fall of Famous Felines: From Grumpy Cat to Smushyface

    b. Dog versus Cat: the Battle Continues, from the Internet to the Convention Center

    c. Felines Online! Pet Popularity, Feline Fame, and the Internet Age

    d. Cats for Cash: is Feline Fame Really Catsploitation?

Passage 4:

It sometimes seems like controversy over social media is never-ending. (1) Social media helps keep friends and family members in touch, helps transmit important news, from weather alerts to updates from warzones, out to the community and to the world, and provides opportunities for businesses to promote their products and reach new customers. (2) However, it also puts vulnerable people at risk, especially teenagers. (3) Cyber-bullying is on the rise, with sad stories of teenage depression and even suicide as a result of it appearing in the news. (4)

Vulnerable people can connect with people in similar difficult circumstances through Facebook groups, online forums, and other sources to find support. (5) Anonymous meeting points are especially helpful for people who are in recovery from mental illnesses like depression or eating disorders; they can confide in other people who have suffered from the same diseases and find the support they need. (6) Not everyone has access to counseling or the means to afford it; perhaps some forms of social media could be a stopgap solution for those in need. (7) Still, there is always the risk of "trolls," people who join these groups only to bully and shame people who really need help. (8)

17. Which sentence best completes the first paragraph in order to create a good transition between two paragraphs?
    a. Social media might do more harm than good in a cruel, unpredictable world; the anonymous world of the internet only brings out the worst in people, and we all must do our part to protect the most vulnerable.
    b. Many people argue that despite its uses, some restrictions should be placed on social media, especially the larger, more influential outlets like Facebook and Twitter.
    c. It might be said that social media is a two-edged sword, something that can enable supportive interaction but also risk facilitating hurtful, abusive behavior.
    d. The tragic stories of cyber-bullying only show that age limits should be placed on social media and even internet use; clearly, teenagers are unable to make good decisions when it comes to social situations, and the anonymity of the internet only enables abusive behavior.

18. What would be the best way to rewrite sentence 5?
    a. No change
    b. Many people who suffer from mental illnesses are isolated and vulnerable to cyber-bullying; social media can provide forums where they can find support from others in similar positions.
    c. It is hard for people who struggle with cyber-bullying because they might also suffer from mental illnesses and therefore feel very alone. With social media, they can connect with other people who also suffer from mental illnesses and form online support groups.
    d. Thanks to the anonymity of the internet, people can stay anonymous and still use social media to connect with other people and find support so they don't feel so alone.

19. What sentence would best follow sentence 8?

    a. Unfortunately the internet is plagued by trolls; finding respite from bullies online even in safe zones set up for the vulnerable is nearly impossible, so members of such groups or sites must remain vigilant and enforce rules about what constitutes abusive behavior.

    b. Fortunately, in these supportive environments, the bullied can become bullies themselves and drive the trolls away – a fate they deserve.

    c. No one is sure how the word *trolls* came to describe online bullies, but it is surely a title they deserve; hiding behind anonymity in order to hurt other people's feelings is nothing to be proud of.

    d. Thanks to online moderators, people may only join supportive online communities after a rigorous screening process, including background checks.

20. Some people feel very isolated or ashamed of mental illnesses or emotional conditions, to the point where they are not comfortable seeking out help, or do not know where to turn to get it; fears of criticism, being thought of as "crazy", losing friends, jobs, and other stigma may prevent them from pursuing therapy or treatment.

    Where would this sentence best be placed in the draft essay?

    a. after sentence 3

    b. after sentence 7

    c. before sentence 5

    d. after sentence 5

Passage 5:

To stay or not to stay? (1) That is the question that faces many high school students as they consider colleges. (2) Whether to attend a college far from home depends on a variety of factors, from cost to personal preference, from opportunities at home to connections around the country or even around the world. (3)

Cost and family are two important factors. One student from Louisiana won a full scholarship to a school in California. (4) So even though she was admitted to several nearby schools in her home state, it was cheaper for her to move across the country, even though she would be far from her family. (5) Another student chose to stay home in Wisconsin and attend a state school for a year in order to save money on tuition and room and board; following his freshman year, he was able to apply to his out-of-state dream school in Chicago and could afford three years away from home. (6)

21. Which sentence <u>best</u> starts the second paragraph in order to create a good transition between two paragraphs?
    a. A recent study of several students across the nation revealed some of the reasons students chose to leave home or stay there for their college years.
    b. The sheer size of the United States provides limitless opportunities for young people seeking a university education; fifty states and six time zones gives students – even those without passports – a lot of options.
    c. Some states, like Texas and California, are so big in terms of geographic size and population that it is possible for a student to attend a great school without even leaving his or her home state.
    d. It can be hard for many students to leave their home region because of the many cultural differences found across our country, but it is a great learning experience for young people in the long term.

22. What would be the <u>best</u> example to use to develop the second paragraph?
    a. a student who travels from Florida to South America to learn Spanish for a year before attending university in Texas, in order to better prepare to major in Latin American studies
    b. a student from North Carolina who chooses to study in Arizona because her aunt and uncle live there; she is familiar with the state and can live with them for her first year of college
    c. a student from Maine who is considering college but plans to join the military after high school
    d. a student who wins a sports scholarship and so attends a university to play on its football team

23. What would be a good way to open a third paragraph of this essay?

    a. Surely, it is important for students to follow their dreams, even if they must ignore their families' wishes and go to college in another state.

    b. Other factors students took into account were their academic and professional interests, seeking out schools that specialized in their chosen career paths or that had the best facilities and professors in their fields.

    c. Some students were willing to stay at home and work, even if it meant waiting a year or two to begin their studies.

    d. A tiny minority of students believed it was more important to get married and have children than to go to college, but only a few respondents reported this belief.

24. Review sentence 5:

So even though she was admitted to several nearby schools in her home state, it was cheaper for her to move across the country, even though she would be far from her family. (5)

What would be the <u>best</u> way to rewrite this sentence?

    a. Even though she had a lot of opportunities in her home state because she could go to college there and live with her family, she went across the country because it was cheaper, since she had a scholarship.

    b. It was cheaper for her to move across the country, even though she was admitted to several nearby schools, and even though she would be far from home.

    c. Despite being accepted to several nearby schools, it was cheaper for her to move across the country.

    d. Despite her acceptance to several nearby schools, it was cheaper for her to move across the country.

Passage 6:

Americans continue to debate the merits of legalizing drugs. (1) Although many states have decriminalized the possession of marijuana, and some have outright legalized it altogether, still others retain harsh penalties for its consumption. (2) There are no easy answers here. (3)

In some states, citizens have agreed on a policy of allowing the use of marijuana for therapeutic purposes. (4) Medical marijuana is used to treat a variety of ailments, and can be obtained with a prescription. (5) It has helped many people suffering from serious afflictions, like cancer, with chronic pain and other conditions. (6) More research must be done in order to uncover any other uses for the drug in medicine. (7) Still, detractors from medical marijuana fear that any level of legal tolerance for the drug is unsafe. (8) Their fears are not entirely unfounded. (9) There is ample evidence to suggest that people who struggle with drug addiction began by abusing marijuana. (10) This may not be a risk for all users, though. (11)

25. Which sentence best replaces sentence 3 in order to provide more clarity and better transition between the two paragraphs?
    a. For many states, a solution lies somewhere in the middle.
    b. Legalizing the use of marijuana for some purposes has been a solution agreed upon in a number of states.
    c. Several states have found consensus by legalizing marijuana for a limited number of uses.
    d. For sure, outright legalization is not the solution at the federal level.

41. Which sentence would best open the second paragraph?
    a. One compromise has been to legalize marijuana for use in medicine and healing.
    b. Some doctors believe in medical marijuana.
    c. It has been proven that in small doses, marijuana can be medically beneficial.
    d. Not all Americans believe that marijuana should be legal for medical uses, but it is still used in medicine in some states.

42. Read this sentence:

More research must be done in order to uncover any other uses for the drug in medicine. (7)

What is the best way to rewrite it?

a. However, more research must be done in order to determine whether there are further therapeutic uses for marijuana.
b. In this case, it is clear that no further research is needed as to the efficacy of medical marijuana, and research would be better spent on cures to these diseases.
c. It is possible that it may have other uses in medicine as well; further research may lead to more information.
d. Without further research, there would be no need to prescribe medical marijuana.

43. What would be the best way to rewrite sentences 8-10?
a. Still, detractors from medical marijuana fear that any level of legal tolerance for the drug is unsafe, and their fears are not entirely unfounded; there is evidence to suggest that people who struggle with drug addiction began by abusing marijuana.
b. Still, detractors from medical marijuana fear that any level of legal tolerance for the drug is unsafe; their fears are not entirely unfounded, there is ample evidence to suggest that people who struggle with drug addiction began by abusing marijuana.
c. Enemies of medical marijuana are afraid that tolerating it is not safe, because they have evidence that drug addicts become addicted to marijuana and spiral out of control quickly.
d. Those who disapprove of legalization of medical marijuana fear that its legalization is unsafe, and for good reason: there is evidence that most drug addicts become addicted by smoking marijuana and get worse quickly.

Passage 6:

Renting your first apartment can be an exhilarating undertaking, but it is also a nerve-wracking experience. (1) There are several issues to consider, like whether to have a roommate, what kind of neighborhood to live in, or whether it is important that you have access to parking or public transportation. (2) However, budget is usually at the top of the list. (3)

You should keep in mind that upon signing a lease, landlords will require a deposit in addition to the first month's rent. (4) Some landlords even require first and last month's rent in addition to the deposit at the time of signing, so be prepared to fork over a lot of money, depending on where you live, because that requirement can vary by state, city, even from building to building. (5) But budget extends beyond just the costs at lease-signing. (6) You might run across your dream apartment, but only be able to afford it if it is in a dangerous neighborhood. (7) In that case, you may need to sacrifice that dream (or at least put it off for a few years) for safety, and find a place to live in a safer area even if that place is smaller than you wanted. (8)

44. Which sentence should be inserted before sentence 4 to begin the second paragraph, in order to ensure the best transition between the two paragraphs?
    a. Be prepared to spend a considerable amount of money just to sign a lease in the first place.
    b. Landlords have varying expectations.
    c. Some landlords are more flexible than others, and you can usually count on them to be understanding in case you cannot afford the apartment you want right away.
    d. You don't always have to sign a lease to rent a place to live, but you might have to.

45. Read the following sentence from the text:

Some landlords even require first and last month's rent in addition to the deposit at the time of signing, so be prepared to fork over a lot of money, depending on where you live, because that requirement can vary by state, city, even from building to building. (5)

What would be the most clear and concise way to rewrite this sentence?

   a. Depending on the state, city, or even building where you are renting, the landlord may require first and last month's rent in addition to the deposit at the time of signing, so be prepared for high move-in costs.
   b. Different landlords in different states, cities, even buildings, may demand first and last month's rent in addition to the deposit at the time of signing, so plan to spend a lot of money, because you might have to!
   c. Landlords in certain states, cities, even certain buildings, may expect first and last month's rent in addition to the deposit at the time of signing, so be prepared to spend a considerable amount of money to move in to a new apartment.
   d. Be prepared for high move-in costs: depending on the state, city, or even building where you are moving, the landlord may expect not only a deposit and the first month's rent, but the last month's rent, too.

46. What sentence would best begin a new paragraph after paragraph 2?
   a. Speaking of neighborhood, outside of budget, choosing an area to live in depends on things like where you work or go to school, what activities you enjoy, and whether you own a car or use public transportation.
   b. It doesn't really matter where you live as long as it is safe and affordable – especially in your first apartment, it is better to be safe than sorry.
   c. Choosing where to live depends on budget, but it can also depend on where you work or attend school, whether you own a car or require public transportation, and what kinds of activities you enjoy.
   d. Even if you can afford to live in an area that you like, it makes more sense to spend as little as possible on your first apartment and save as much money as you can; you can always live somewhere nicer when you are older.

47. What would be the <u>best</u> sentence to add after sentence 1?
   a. It can be fun to search for housing, but dealing with landlords, realtors and rules about leasing can be stressful.
   b. Thinking about getting a roommate, how much money you have to spend, or talking to landlords—these are serious considerations.
   c. You might even want to consider getting a real estate agent.
   d. However, for some people, the stress can be part of the fun!

Passage 7:

Traveling on commercial airlines has changed substantially <u>over years</u>. (1) When commercial air travel first became available, it was so expensive that usually only businessmen could afford <u>to do so</u>. Airplane efficiency, the relative cost of fossil fuels, <u>and using economies</u> of scale have all contributed to make travel by air more affordable and common. These days, there are nearly 30,000 commercial air flights in the world each day!

Depending on the size of the airport you are departing from, you should arrive 90 minutes to two and a half hours before your plane leaves. Things like checking your luggage and flying internationally can make the process of getting to your gate take longer. If you fly out of a very busy airport, like <u>LaGuardia, in</u> New York City, on a very busy travel day, like the day before Thanksgiving, you can easily miss your flight if you don't arrive early enough.

Security processes for passengers have also changed. In the 1960s, there was <u>hardly any</u> security: you could just buy your ticket and walk on to the plane the day of the flight without even needing to show identification. In the 1970s, American commercial airlines started installing sky marshals on many <u>flights, an</u> undercover law enforcement officers who would protect the passengers from a potential hijacking.

Also in the early 1970s, the federal government began to require that airlines screen passengers and their luggage for things like weapons and bombs. After the 2001 terrorist attacks in the United States, these requirements were <u>stringently enforced</u>. Family members can no longer meet someone at the gate<u>; only ticketed passengers are allowed into the gate area</u>. The definition of <u>weapons are</u> not allowed is expanded every time there is a new incident for example liquids are now restricted on planes after an attempted planned attack using gel explosives in 2006.

Despite the hassles of traveling by air, it is still a boon to modern <u>life. Still, some </u>businesses are moving away from sending employees on airplane trips, <u>as</u> face-to-face video conferencing technologies improve. A trip which might take ten hours by car <u>can take only</u> two hours by plane. However, the ability to travel quickly by air <u>will always be valued, by citizens</u> of our modern society.

48. Which of the following is the best change to the underlined portion of sentence 1?

   a. No Change.
   b. "over the years"
   c. "over time"
   d. Delete.

49. Which of the following is the best change to the underlined portion of sentence 2?

   a. No Change.
   b. "to do it"
   c. "to fly"
   d. "do so"

50. Which of the following is the best change to the underlined portion of sentence 3?

   a. No Change.
   b. "using economies"
   c. "and the use of economies"
   d. "and economies"

51. Which of the following is the best change to the underlined portion of sentence 7?

   a. No Change.
   b. "La Guardia in"
   c. "La Guardia; in"
   d. "La Guardia,"

52. Which of the following is the best change to the underlined portion of sentence 7?

   a. No Change.
   b. "hardly"
   c. "no"
   d. "barely'

53. Which of the following is the best change to the underlined portion of sentence 9?

   a. No Change.
   b. "flights; an"
   c. "flights. Marshals are"
   d. "flights, marshals are"

54. Which of the following is the best change to the underlined portion of sentence 11?
    a. No Change.
    b. "stiffly upheld"
    c. "enforced with more stringency"
    d. "more stringently enforced"

55. If the underlined portion in sentence 12 were deleted, the passage would lose:
    a. No Change.
    b. An explanation of the screening process.
    c. Ambiguity over why family members are no longer allowed at the gate.
    d. A further specific example of how regulations have changed over time.

56. Which of the following is the best change to the underlined portion in sentence 13?
    a. No Change.
    b. "weapon is"
    c. "weapons"
    d. "weapons which are"

57. Which of the following is the proper transition between sentences 13 & 14?
    a. No Change.
    b. "life. Some"
    c. "life even though some"
    d. "life, still some"

Practice Test: Writing Prompt

Write an essay in 25 minutes by answering the question from your perspective. Be sure to provide evidence.

- *In The Dispossessed, published in 1974, groundbreaking science fiction author Ursula K. LeGuin wrote, "You can't crush ideas by suppressing them. You can only crush them by ignoring them."*

  Is it possible to get rid of an idea?

Practice Test Answer Key

Reading

1. C.
2. B.
3. D.
4. C.
5. A.
6. A.
7. B.
8. C.
9. D.
10. A.
11. B.
12. D.
13. A.
14. D.
15. D.
16. C.
17. B.
18. A.
19. D.
20. D.
21. A.
22. C.
23. C.
24. B.
25. A.
26. D.
27. B.
28. B.
29. A.
30. C.
31. D.
32. A.
33. B.
34. C.
35. B.
36. D.
37. B.
38. D.
39. B.
40. C.

Mathematics

1. D.	20. B.
2. D.	21. C.
3. A.	22. C.
4. B.	23. B.
5. B.	24. C.
6. B.	25. C.
7. A.	26. C.
8. D.	27. D.
9. C.	28. A.
10. D.	29. D.
11. C.	30. A.
12. D.	31. B.
13. B.	32. B.
14. C.	33. B.
15. D.	34. A.
16. A.	35. D.
17. B	36. A.
18. B.	37. B.
19. B.	38. D.
	39. D.
	40. C.

Writing

1. A.	23. B.
2. D.	24. D.
3. C.	25. C.
4. C.	26. A.
5. D.	27. C.
6. D.	28. A.
7. B.	29. A.
8. D.	30. D.
9. D.	31. C.
10. C.	32. A.
11. B.	33. B.
12. A.	34. C.
13. A.	35. C.
14. C.	36. B.
15. D.	37. A.
16. C.	38. C.
17. C.	39. D.
18. B.	40. D.
19. A.	41. D.
20. D.	42. C.
21. A.	
22. B.	

Writing Prompt

Score of 5+:

The suppression of ideas has been attempted over and over throughout history by different oppressive regimes. This theme has been explored as well in literature, through such dystopian works as 1984 and Fahrenheit 454. But these histories and stories always play out the same way: eventually, the repressed idea bubbles to the surface and triumphs. Ursula K. LeGuin acknowledged this by saying that ideas can be crushed not by suppression, but by omission.

In Aldous Huxley's novel Brave New World, the world government maintains order not by governing people strictly and policing their ideas, but by distracting them. Consumption is the highest value of the society. When an outsider ot the society comes in and questions it, he is exiled—not to punish him, but to remove his influence from society. The government of the dystopia has learned that the best way to maintain control is to keep citizens unaware of other, outside ideas. This theme resonates with a modern audience more than other, more authoritarian tales of dystopia because in our society, we are less controlled than we are influenced and persuaded.

Repressing ideas through harsh authoritarian rule has proven time and again to be ultimately fruitless. For example, in Soviet Russia during the 1920s and 1930s, Josef Stalin attempted to purge his society of all religious belief. This was done through suppression: discriminatory laws were enacted, members of the clergy were executed, and the religious citizenry were terrified. While these measures drastically crippled religious institutions, they were ineffective at completely eliminating the idea of religion. Beliefs and traditions were passed down in communities clandestinely throughout the repressive rule of Stalin. After the fall of the Soviet Union, it became clear that religion had survived all along.

We see throughout literature and history that ignoring ideas and distracting people from them is generally more effective than to attempt to stamp an idea out through means of suppression. Authoritarian rule, in fact, can do the opposite: by dramatizing and calling attention to an idea in the name of condemning it, a regime might actually strengthen that idea.

Score of 3-4:

We have seen different governments try to crush out ideas throughout history. However, they are never actually successful in doing so. An idea can be ignored or suppressed, but it will never really go away. This is illustrated in the survival of religion in the Soviet Union.

In Soviet Russia during the 1920s and 1930s, Josef Stalin attempted to purge the society of all religious belief. This was done through suppression: discriminatory laws, execution of the clergy, and use of terror. While this harmed religious institutions, they were ineffective at crushing the idea of religion. Beliefs and traditions were passed down in communities secretly throughout the rule of Stalin. After the fall of the Soviet Union, it became clear that religion had survived all along.

The same kind of thing happened with apartheid law in South Africa. Even though there were laws against black Africans and white Africans using the same facilities, the idea caught fire, especially because of an international outcry against the law.

We see throughout history that suppressing ideas does not crush them. Authoritarian rule, in fact, can do the opposite: by calling attention to an idea in the name of condemning it, a regime might actually strengthen that idea.

Score of 2 or Less:

It is not possible to crush out an idea by ignoring it or by suppressing it. All throughout history, whenever anyone has tried to do this, they might be temporarily successful but the idea will always survive or come back. For example in the Soviet Union religion was suppressed. People were not allowed to practice their religion. But after the government fell, religion still existed – people had held on to their ideas during the time of suppression.